ANGEL
IN
GOD'S OFFICE

For Anna and John

ANGEL IN GOD'S OFFICE

MY WARTIME DIARIES

Neva Clarke McKenna

TANDEM PRESS

First published in New Zealand in 1996 by
TANDEM PRESS
2 Rugby Road, Birkenhead, North Shore City,
New Zealand

Copyright © 1996 Neva Clarke McKenna

ISBN 0 908884 85 0

Cover design by Christine Hansen
Design and production by Graeme Leather
Printed and bound by Australian Print Group

A PART OF me has always felt it would be wishy-washy to write of what is inside me because it would mean revealing emotions, and my generation was taught to keep these to ourselves. All along I've secretly known that the cause of these emotions was so serious, so important to us all, that they deserved to be aired, but I was afraid and embarrassed until recently to tell my story. Although I am too advanced in years now to be either embarrassed or afraid, I am far too sceptical to imagine this book will alter the thinking of anyone with power or ambition. All I can do is give of myself and hope a spark will flicker in someone somewhere.

An occasional episode too good to omit from this book has been attributed to other than the instigator. This obviated introducing further characters and perhaps weakening the important aspects of my story. I offer my apologies to those others who nevertheless will remain in my memory as part of a strangely enriching experience.

Neva Clarke McKenna

1
CHAPTER

I SEE SUE'S tea-towel hanging out her kitchen window. She was sure it would be visible as we left the harbour and she was right. I wave, which is ridiculous, as from where she is there is no way she can recognise one person in this blob of khaki, but I feel impelled. Does she know how I feel leaving for the war as Geoff had, I wonder? Does she recall, as she watches, the day we saw him off? I wonder that too. Damn that tea-towel. It interferes with what is happening around me.

We've been waiting for months to sail, being sent home from Miramar camp three times on final leave because of submarine scares, then returning to Wellington to temporary jobs in the city. But now, on a clear morning early in 1944, we are on our way.

The staff of Sick and Wounded where I have been working are there on the wharf below waving. Suddenly I am overwhelmed, not wanting to leave New Zealand at all, but I am jolted out of this by an announcement from the loud speaker. 'Will the WAAC from Gisborne please report to the Purser's office.' All the girls look at me, the WAAC from Gisborne.

Crowded in the Purser's office is the Minister of Defence, along with other Members of Parliament, and an officer from the Gisborne Army Office, there to see his Ngatiporou boys off. Such excitement as he squeezes the breath from me! How dare he be so Maorily handsome!

Our little ship, the *Ruys*, is staffed partly by Javanese, whose ages are hard to guess. All we are sure of is that they are between 15 and 50 and are clean and capable and black. Tonight, the one who waits on our table gave me an extra apple to take to our cabin which six of us share, three Aucklanders who know one another well, a girl from the deep south, and Nancy and myself. I know Nancy a little. She worked in Napier and we met en route to Wellington to report to Army Headquarters, where we were both volunteering to go overseas in the Clerical Division of the New Zealand Women's Auxiliary Army Corps. (NZWAAC). We were allotted to the same hut in Miramar Camp, so when I say

I know her a little, this is not entirely true. I know how quick or slow her movements are (they are never hurried); I know whether she sleeps in a straight line or with her knees bent (she lies on her back and seldom moves all night); I know if her appetite is large or small (it is large); I know if she is co-operative (she is when it pleases her, depending on whether or not she likes the person with whom she is supposed to co-operate). Nancy is very tall and dark and has blue eyes; she is very firm, but I suspect a softness underneath. She is also very intelligent and very funny.

Most of our group come direct from civilian life, but others, like myself, have been in the Army for two years and more. My being in the Army at all was a mistake, which I'll tell you about later. For the purposes of serving overseas I willingly dropped my three sergeant's stripes and reverted to private as was decreed.

Sending girls away in the Clerical Division of New Zealand WAACs is an experiment on the part of the Army. Already girls are serving overseas in the Medical Division as nursing sisters and voluntary aids in our military hospitals, and others, known as Tuis, are in the Welfare Division and work in our New Zealand clubs. Now it has been deemed appropriate to send girls to administrative headquarters as secretaries. We have been assured that each of our small group has been carefully selected so our expertise at least can not be criticised. The main concern is that the male office workers will resent the possibility of our replacing them. Will this be so, we wonder?

ON BOARD SHIP we are busy having more tetanus and typhoid injections, although we already had these before leaving New Zealand. Those of us whose smallpox vaccinations had not taken have now had our sixth. This means only Nancy and myself. She grew up on a dairy farm, and my parents have a house cow, Prudence, so perhaps we two are immune to smallpox.

Most of the girls do not work while on board. But an officer returning from furlough has commandeered me, firstly to up-date his copy of King's Regulations — a painstaking job I loathe. I have finished that, so he now dictates personal stories to me about his experiences in Egypt, much of the time in brothels. As he dictates his cheeks grow an excited shade of pink while I am straight-faced. I don't enjoy knowing the size and shape of his penis and what he does with it, or what he and the girls say to each other. As I tell Nan, you'd think he had invented sexual intercourse. Why don't I simply leave him and join the other girls? Because he's a major, that's why. There was a time I thought doctors and lawyers and senior officers in His Majesty's services were close to being God, but that was a while ago.

When I finish making shorthand notes about the major's penis, I sunbathe with the other girls on a small section of deck set aside for our use. Someone is obviously concerned for our safety and/or morals and insists that over our shorts we wear a smock when walking to our designated spot lest in passing we upset the boys. As far as we can see, they look anything but upset. To us this seems a weird rule, and as a protest we smile widely at the soldiers we pass. There is no rule against smiling.

Days pass nicely. I have vague squirmy feelings from time to time, but a naval officer assures me that the sea is not rough. I think him eccentric, otherwise why would he be anxious to teach me not only the Russian but the Braille alphabet? The first is understandable. I have been questioned about my name, Neva, and tell anyone interested that it is Russian, which is true, and that my real name is Nevoska Wisnorgsky, which is not true. As a result two things have happened. Each day the linguist gives me an exercise in Russian to decipher. That is one thing. The other is equally strange. Someone has printed 'Nevoska Wisnorgsky' on the side of a lifeboat, with the traditional heart and arrow alongside.

It is obvious that deciphering a Braille exercise will bring more amused looks than deciphering a message in Russian but my tutor and I pretend we do not know what these looks imply. When I tell him I almost feel seasick, he gives me a Braille exercise, 'Repeat after me, it is almost a flat calm.'

Our purser, a Dutchman, hands me a copy of a long poem demonstrating the difficulty of learning English. It begins:

Dearest creature in creation
Studying English pronunciation
I will teach you in my verse
Sounds like corpse, corps, horse and worse

After reading three pages of this, I concede that he is doing well telling me, 'You is always heppy and wants to be more enjoyable.' I think I know what he means.

Men like my Lecherous Major (I shall call him L.M. from now on) should not be on board, should not, after serving for three years and having been home on furlough, be sent back into action. How do they feel, I wonder, as they look at us, talk to us, people who do not know what they know about war and have

3

no way of imagining it? Perhaps they despise us. I am careful in their company, careful not to be frivolous, though I try to be cheerful. I am getting closer to asking one of them how he feels about returning, how painful it is to consider, how terrifying even. I look around the lounge and decide who it will be that I approach. Will it be the captain, who is teaching us the words of 'Lili Marlene'? (We have just been told we are not going to the Pacific Islands, as we had been led to believe, but to the Middle East, and it is apparently essential that we know the words of this song if we are to be anywhere near Germans.) But no, it will not be the captain. I think it will be the lieutenant who always sits in the corner by a palm tree. He reads and reads, but sometimes I notice, without his noticing, that he puts down his book and looks straight ahead wearing such sadness I almost can not bear to watch him. I think he will be the one because I sense that I have been wherever he is in his mind; perhaps, in a different way, I have been in that lonely place.

There are two rascals from the Free French Forces amongst us, and a third who possibly is not a rascal and who speaks only two words of English. At breakfast he smiles. 'Good morning', he says. And as he leaves the lounge in the evening, he smiles again. 'Good morning,' he says. And we say 'Good morning' in return as we don't like to hurt his feelings. His fellow Frenchmen speak passable English, are outrageous flirts and cheat at cards. Undressing me with his eyes, one asks me why we English measure the land in feet and the water in fathoms, and before I can conjure up a reply adds, 'I sink ze Eenglish are afraid of getting ze feet wet.'

Many of the men below are really seasick, and most of us in our cabins have prickly heat. Each night, just before dark, a small Javanese sailor enters our cabin to black out the porthole. Tonight before going to dinner one of our girls had just finished her wash-all-over in front of the hand-basin and was balanced, one foot raised ready to put into her panties, when the Javanese steward opened the door and walked in. The girl screeched and pulled her panties over her head! The Javanese crossed the cabin with admirable nonchalance, attached the blackout screen and was gone. We others laughed and laughed as the girl hurried into the toilet, her panties in her hand, but when she did not emerge for some time Nancy and I exchanged a glance. After the other three left for the dining room, we knocked on the toilet door. With a towel clutched about her, the girl opened the door and slowly came out.

'We're sorry,' Nan and I said simultaneously.

4

'I was so embarrassed I could have died. What will I do when I see him again? He must have told all the others what he saw.'

'You needn't worry,' I told her gently. 'The only thing he didn't see was your face.'

Something has occurred to me. Of all the girls on board I am the only one who sees anyone from her home town. In the officers' lounge, which we use, there are two Gisbornites, both of whom I know well, and today from our sunbathing area I looked down at a lower deck and saw a man who had worked in our post office. Cupping my hands I called in a loud whisper, 'Hello, Gisborne George,' and three Gisborne men named George waved to me. And on Sunday there were church services — Anglican, Catholic and Presbyterian. I went to the Presbyterian, and sitting on the floor in a puddle of perspiration along with several Gisbornites I felt closer to heaven than I'd ever felt in church at home dressed up in Sunday best.

After being down below to the service I felt seedy, but the linguist said ominously, 'Wait till we get to the Australian Bight.' I think I'm pleased he is joining his own ship at Fremantle and I can thereafter form my own opinion on rough seas. Tonight I translated his Braille message, 'It is not rough. The sea is very calm.' At the foot of the answer I added a question, 'If the sea is so calm, where does all the spray come from?'

The Javanese steward has given me a pear tonight instead of an apple, but I gave it to the girl who threw her panties over her head.

We are practising for a concert. We girls are to sing a Negro spiritual and 'Coming in on a Wing and a Prayer', and there will be Maori songs too. Someone has decided that the descants and solo sections are to be sung by me, not because I sing magnificently, but because the other girls are worse.

WE'VE FINISHED WITH the Australian Bight, thank goodness, and are about to turn around the bottom left-hand corner of Australia. A lot of men have given us ironing to do prior to their being let loose in Perth, where they want to look as handsome as possible. We girls are told we must wear our dress uniform — thick khaki serge, with thick khaki woollen stockings and a thick khaki felt hat — when what we would prefer to wear in this heat is our skin. For security reasons we are to remove our New Zealand tabs from our epaulettes.

At around morning-tea time we go ashore. The linguistic naval officer is transferring to the *Suffolk* today but is spending time with a gaggle of us from the

Ruys for lunch at the Esplanade Hotel. A sheep and wheat farming couple with 10,000 acres north of Perth kindly ask us all to visit them, but there is no time. We WAACs are bundled into trucks and taken to an artillery beach defence post, then on to an Australian Women's Army camp at Cottesloe.

If hell is as hot as this place I'd be surprised, and compared with New Zealand camps the conditions are primitive. These girls live in tents, their baths are made of tin, there is little in the way of sewerage and the cooks use coal ranges. There is no grass, only sand 10 centimetres deep. The staff would think themselves princesses if they could work at Miramar camp with all its cleanliness and order, its gleaming kitchen, its stainless steel everything. Cameras must be registered at this camp so I register mine, then take snaps of some of these hot, perspiring and underprivileged army slaves.

Back in Perth for dinner, we meet some of the boys off the *Ruys* who mistake us for Australians. One claims that their New Zealand girls are second to none and we heartily agree. When we divulge our identity they are furious to know we are off the same ship as themselves.

Early next morning we pull out from Fremantle with a band playing. The sea is truly flat for the first time since leaving home, but there are some on board as bad as the linguist. Wait till we get to the Indian Ocean, they warn, wait till the monsoons hit us. The *Suffolk* and a large French ship full of Americans are alongside us; there is also a warship and a lot of aircraft. Lifeboat drill is serious now and we have a nightly roll-call.

On this, our first night out, my L.M. and another officer have almost come to blows over the wisdom or otherwise of visiting brothels. The air is thick and they are not speaking.

We have our first race meeting. The course is a long roll of canvas marked out into spaces and the horses are small metal toys. In turn, each horse owner throws a dice and moves his horse forward the appropriate number of spaces. The Maiden Stakes are won by 'Dark Love' by 'Longing' out of 'Dark Thoughts'; the Reveille Handicap is won by 'Rude Awakening' by 'Orderly Officer' out of 'Hammock'; the Ship's Scurry is won by 'Knitted Tie' by 'Woo' out of 'Who'; and the All Comers Mixed Scramble is won by 'Nose Dive' out of 'Bunk'.

A padre is teaching us Italian. Or trying to. He is very intent on grammar, in which few of us are interested. We appear to prefer nouns and verbs and nothing else and I feel he will despair of us. He is short and round and totally unstimulating, and is so earnest we can't concentrate. I wonder if he is any more successful as a padre and wish I didn't have to feel sorry for him, but am obliged to because we are all such dreadful students and behave so appallingly in the classroom.

My apple and pear steward's name is Oscar. He told me. Because I asked.

The other girls don't seem to ask questions the way I do. I think I am like cattle running towards you with their myopic eyes when you enter their field. Curious. I blame my father for my curiosity. When tiny and toddling around as his shadow, I wanted to know about everything he was doing. As he weeded onions one day he told me what it was like growing up as an Orangeman in Ulster, and I asked if there were Catholic ants and Protestant ants. He said probably not, but that there would be groups of ants that fought just as people do. Then he paused and said, 'Nugget, never stop asking questions. They're more important than answers, because there wouldn't be any answers if you didn't ask questions.' I found this confusing, but even more confusing was that at another time he told me that if I kept my mouth closed and my ears open I would always learn something.

Puzzled, I asked, 'How can I ask questions with my mouth closed?'

'As you grow older you'll be able to decide when to do which,' he said.

My parents seemed always to give convoluted replies to my questions. So when I asked the steward his name and he quietly slipped some grapes beside my plate and said, 'Oscar', a huge surge of gratitude overwhelmed me. I expected him to tell me why he was called Oscar, that it was after his father or a very-dead forbear or a character from a novel, and that he had a brother called Hadrian after the wall and a sister called Mermaid, which his mother did not like. I was pleased with the simplicity of his reply, 'Oscar'. It had a wholesomeness about it, so that I could roll the name around on my tongue and enjoy it.

Later I asked Nancy why on earth a Javanese parent would name a son Oscar. Without hesitation she said that Oscar was his real name Racso in reverse and his father had been inebriated when registering the birth. I can always bank on Nan having a reply worth considering.

We have just passed a buoy marking the spot where a ship was sunk, and twice today we have been called to boat stations with our lifejackets on. The rest of the time I have been typing for my L.M., who is still recounting his tales of brothels.

There was time off for a concert rehearsal. A BBC performer who is reputed to have written 'Blueberry Hill' is in charge. With him is a short, ginger-haired man who sings like a past-his-prime Nelson Eddy.

We have also had a short lecture by an Australian group captain, 'Bombing over Germany', which I found disturbing.

We were being taken over the innards of the ship, with engines and plumbing and other imponderables being explained to us, when there was an Action Station alert (more than four rings of a bell) followed by Boat Stations (a continual clanging), and we shot to our cabins for our life jackets. It seemed a lifetime till four rings announced the All Clear. The *Suffolk* is still alongside, which brings a certain comfort because we are apparently in dangerous waters and are very vulnerable.

Five of us have birthdays close together and tomorrow the purser is putting on a party for us in his office because someone told him it was a good idea. It was probably Nan.

Yesterday we crossed the line and were given a souvenir card by King Neptune. I had the captain of the ship sign mine because I like to know who captains the ships I am on. But his signature is illegible, perhaps because he is Dutch, so I still don't know who he is.

We have just had an Anzac Service. I felt so miserable, and my throat and chest ached through holding back tears. To make things worse, a Wellington bomber flew over us. I wish I was at home with Mum and Dad.

2
CHAPTER

WE CAN LOOK at Aden. Only the purser and the Australian group captain have gone ashore. How can anyone live in such heat as this? Yet I see a teeming mass of natives on a hillside. Some buildings on the waterfront are arched, while beyond them are others of grey stone, barely distinguishable from the steep cliffs on which they are built. Native boys are loading coal into a ship nearby at a fast rate, and from the shore others are pulling boats along, Volga-boatman fashion. With apparent disdain a camel trudges along the foreshore.

A group of young boys paddle out to our ship in a canoelike craft, bringing a load of brightly coloured wares they hope we will buy. When all haggling is over they dive for coins, copper to begin with, but later only for silver.

We now have what we call brownout rather than blackout, but find it no less hot. It is not surprising to learn that in army terms two years' service counts as five in this strange place which has an airfield and huge salt mines and heat, heat, heat.

We have just exchanged our money for local currency and been up on the bridge to view the Twelve Apostle Islands and eat ice cream. This is possibly the reason the purser and the group captain went ashore, to buy the ice cream.

At a concert a Maori wiggles in front of us to the amusement of the other dancers, so I assume the wiggle was sexual. One of our girls obliges by doing a beautiful hula and is the hit of the show when her skirt falls off. The concert is followed by a church service on deck where God is thanked by three padres for our safe voyage. Then there is a race meeting at which I lose the equivalent of twopence.

WE ARE IN the Red Sea en route to Tewfik, the port of Cairo. Passing Australian troopships is good for a lot of waving and shouting. The chief Tui from the New Zealand Club in Cairo comes on board when we dock, stunningly beautiful in her uniform, making us feel like country cousins with our crumpled look, our drill jackets worn without blouses underneath and our dreadful woollen stockings. Hers are nylon.

The water here is vivid blue and the harbour is full of small ships, large ships, fat ships and thin ships. As we prepare to go ashore by barge there are kisses and hugs for the men we have to come to know and for some we have not come to know. Among the watching crew is Oscar. He winks wickedly when he catches my glance, and I understand that the extra fruit which came my way is a secret we share. I wink back as wickedly as I am able.

On shore the first New Zealander we see is a Gisbornite. 'Of course,' chorus the girls. He guides us to ambulances, in which we travel to the rest home in Cairo's Garden City, once a Pasha's palace. Such a road through a hundred miles of desert, but sealed at least through the endless sand.

I am in a room with two others and Nan is next door with another two. Some girls are underground, maybe where the Pasha kept his harem.

The doctor has been here giving another tetanus and typhoid jab to us all, and for Nan and me another smallpox vaccination, number seven. Almost immediately I feel ill, but stagger with the others on a conducted tour to the Pyramids and the Sphinx and other interesting places I would like to see if I could keep my eyes open. Later I go to dinner with my L.M., but half way through the meal he takes me back to the rest home to die. The doctor comes. 'This girl must go to hospital right away,' he says, devoid of passion.

Two days later I am back at the rest home, to be told that a few of us will work at Maadi Camp but that most, including Nan and myself, have been posted to Santo Spirito in Southern Italy. There is outfitting to be done, and a last rush of sightseeing and shopping before we leave in the morning.

Yesterday afternoon I went sightseeing with a South African we met on a tour. Later, when we went to the South African Club and my escort disappeared to change from shorts to longs at sunset, two men approached me.

'Do you speak Greek?' they wanted to know.

'No, not Greek,' I said, slightly emphasising the word 'Greek', indicating that this was my only linguistic failing.

When he returned looking glamourous, the South African explained that these men were high-ranking true Greeks, and he was not only puzzled but obviously annoyed at their approaching me. I feel he might constitute a slight problem in my life. Given the chance of course.

Perhaps this is a warning. I had a note from the man on board ship who was returning from furlough, the lieutenant I chose to question about his feelings. But first I'll tell you about that first meeting with him.

Watching him, deciding, I hesitated to speak to him at all, but in me there was something as strong as the something in him, and I knew that approaching him would be all right. It would not be the intrusion I was fearful of and I would be accepted. So I wound through the lounge furniture to where he sat as usual, beneath the fronds of his palm tree.

'Do you mind if I sit here for a while?'

He looked surprised, then gave a small smile I can only describe as sweet, a word I don't like to apply to men. But it was a sweet smile. He was not a tall man, but sat straight in the large chair, adding inches to his height. His eyes were set well apart and were a soft grey like my father's, his hair was fair and his skin a light golden brown. Briefly but firmly he shook my hand. There was a silence.

'What unit are you with?' I asked.

'The 19th.'

'My brother-in-law-to-be was in the 19th,' I said. 'Captured at Alamein.'

'Who is he?'

'Bill Aitken.'

'Good old Bill! He took over the battalion's dog, Major, when Errol Williams was killed.'

'He and Errol made a pact. If Errol was killed, Bill would write to his wife. If Bill was killed, Errol would write to my sister.'

The lieutenant nodded, and there was another silence.

'I'm sorry you're going back,' I said. 'You shouldn't be, you men. You've had enough.'

The officer hung his head briefly.

'I'm sorry,' I said. My Irish emotion welled up inside me and I wanted very much to say something helpful but could think of nothing, so sat waiting.

'I'll tell you something,' the officer said, turning towards me. 'Anyone who says he doesn't mind going back is lying. And we don't forget those bastards at home who've never been away, sitting safe in our jobs while we return to be killed.'

'Oh, God, I hope not.'

'I have a cloak of dread around me and I know I will be.' The man sighed. 'My wife and I have talked of this.' He hesitated, then continued. 'She says if I'm killed she doesn't want to go on living.'

I said, 'I don't want to believe any of this.'

'Let's not be morbid. I don't want to bore you.' The officer's smile was barely a smile. Somehow it hurt me.

'We're talking about things that matter,' I said. 'Maybe the only things that matter — living and dying, loving and . . . I won't say hating. It's a word my father won't allow in our household.' I smiled, remembering. 'We were taught to say we don't like, but not that we hate.'

'You've a good role model then.'

I nodded. 'Couldn't be better.' And we spoke of other things.

And now he writes to me. It was wonderful to talk to another person, he says, to a girl who listened and understood. He is sure I understand how he feels. He says I will never know what I did for him, and that he had wished, as we talked, that the clock could stop for ever. He will tell his wife of our talk, and he knows she will be pleased we met.

He is wrong, of course. His wife will not be pleased to know we've met. He should tell a lie, say it was a male he spoke to, a male who listened and understood. It will be no comfort to his wife to have a letter saying how good it was to talk to a female geographically close to him when she herself is on the other side of the world. It will be a special sort of torture. Before it is too late I must let him know that he is terribly wrong.

This is the lesson I have learned early then: that by simply listening you can have an immediate reaction such as this on a man over here; the possibilities are a little frightening, something to be wary of. I imagine the South African's little green eye will need watching — that is, if we ever meet again. There is that. So much happening, so many uncertainties, perhaps no tomorrows. It doesn't bear thinking of.

IN AMBULANCES WE leave the rest home just after six in the morning, singing, singing, singing 'You are My Sunshine', 'My Beautiful Sarie Marais', 'The Maori Battalion Song', 'The Isle of Capri'. Into Ismalia, out of Ismalia, singing and singing, until we reach Port Said and the Officers' Club for lunch, still singing.

No one can possibly know we are New Zealanders as we have again removed all shoulder flashes and badges for security reasons. Yet every Egyptian we pass shouts 'Goodbye, Kiwi' or 'Good luck, Kiwi'. And at the club we are greeted by an officer resplendent with every sign of identity our Division has ever possessed.

By 2 p.m. we are aboard the *Orion*.

Amongst the disorder about boat and action stations on this British ship, we are equipped with American life jackets. On our Dutch ship they were English. On board with us there is a true mix of nationalities — English, Yugoslav, Czech, Italian, Rhodesian, South African, Greek, Polish, Welsh, Russian and ourselves — 300 New Zealanders.

An enemy sub was sighted today, and we are now told that one chased us in the Red Sea. So we travel, zigging and zagging across the Mediterranean. Filling in time means playing cards, talking, telling endless jokes, laughing a lot, playing unorthodox games with a medicine ball, practising for our item in a forthcoming concert and watching a group of Basutos practising for theirs, eating, entering quiz sessions in which we surprise ourselves with our success, and swallowing mepacrine tablets as a precaution against malaria.

Our last night aboard, and the concert is remarkably rewarding from our point of view. In splendid order an unaccompanied Welsh choir files on stage and with faultless voice control fills the lounge with glorious and moving sound. The clapping is subdued. Then we Kiwis straggle into our allotted places, whisper to our neighbours, smile at those we know in the audience, and sing 'Pokarekare Ana' and 'Haere Ra'. Then we straggle off the stage. The shouting and whistling and stamping are deafening. The English organiser is suitably pleased with us.

In the morning we anchor in Taranto's large harbour, and on 'B' deck we girls wait with our water bottles, gas-masks, respirators and satchels, and a gramophone a lovely Welfare Division girl has lent us. At the New Zealand Club, where she will work, she will have no need for it, so we have it on long-term loan.

We say goodbye to friends, and I decide that of all the nationalities we have met on board I prefer the English.

Our men go ashore first, and then it is our turn to scramble on to the barge with our impedimenta, bumping against gangway rails, rescuing kitbags which have slipped off shoulders and are dragging by our feet, then stepping onto Italian soil. I see a field of bright red poppies.

3

CHAPTER

WHY AM I here in Italy? Why am I in the army? I said I'd tell you about its being a mistake.

You could say it was because I went to a Surf Club Saturday night dance with one of the nicest young men in Gisborne and two other couples. We all belonged to the Mildred Hamilton School of Ballroom Dancing. Perhaps the dancing class is why I ended up in the army, so I'll start there. No. I'll go back further because I would not have joined the ballroom dancing class had it not been for a special thing. I was shy. So, you see, one thing leads to another, backwards in this case. It was my shyness which led to my being in the army. Listen.

I was so shy as a child that I was a pain, one of those awful kids who would not speak when spoken to by almost any adult other than my father and mother. Aunts and uncles were all right, and the boy who delivered our meat was not entirely terrifying, nor the two spinsters next door with their long hair pulled tightly back into buns five centimetres in diameter.

Children at school didn't frighten me, but when the time came to leave high school I was alarmed. This was half way through my third year. The principal called another girl and myself to his office after assembly and said we were to report at the Crown Solicitor's office that afternoon to apply for a job. Neither of us had considered leaving school, and our parents were not consulted, but this was at the tail end of the depression and you didn't ask questions when jobs were mentioned. I rode home on my bicycle and told my mother, and we simply stood. I had nothing to wear. An aunt around the corner arrived with stockings and a pair of shoes the right size, and we searched my sister's wardrobe and found a blouse and skirt. However, I was tiny — under 1.5 metres tall, though I gained 13 centimetres later — and my sister was tall, so my mother and I pinned the hem of the skirt up with dozens of those minute pins. Then, after almost scrubbing my fingernails away because I was assured that getting or not getting the job could depend on this, I rode into town.

It was almost impossible to walk through the office doorway. Inside I was ushered into a large room and seated on one side of an oversized desk. On the other side of the desk sat a row of what looked like owls, the four partners in this legal firm. A part of me whispered not to be afraid because the other girl being interviewed was a year older than I, was quite lovely, had supreme confidence and fine rosy cheeks, and would certainly be chosen. In the morning I'd be back at school. So I sat demurely, answered questions and worried about my fingernails, which were out of sight on my knee where none of the owls could catch a glimpse of them. And for some reason I got the job.

After a week of being almost too afraid to go to work I realised that I was the only one who could do anything about my shyness and I joined the ballroom dancing class. On a Tuesday evening I rode into town, balanced my bicycle against the kerb and climbed a narrow stairway. The brown linoleum on each step was nibbled at the edges as if by mice, adding to my nervous state. At the top of the stairs I looked into a vast room which had mirrors around the bottom of the walls so that as you danced you could see what you were doing wrong with your feet. Across the room a small group of young people huddled, looking as afraid as I. If I could possibly get across to them I might survive, I thought, and somehow I managed this. That night we learned the fundamentals of ballroom dancing — the quarter turn, the natural turn and the reverse turn — and I have never been shy since.

Why do I tell you all this? Because being at that dancing class to cure my shyness led to my being at the Surf Club dance, which led to my falling in love across a crowded room, which, in a strange way, led to my being in the army. His name was Geoff.

All through his primary schooling Geoff had been moved to upper classes and he entered Otago Boys' High School just after his eleventh birthday. He passed his Matriculation examination at only 14.

Such bright pupils are almost always smaller physically than their classmates, and, although he was strong and agile, this was so with Geoff. As a result, team games were not possible for him. Undeterred, he turned to swimming and before long swam a New Zealand record time which remained intact for many years.

On his arrival in Gisborne, Geoff introduced the butterfly stroke to the town, and while I secretly thought it incredibly ugly I glowed with pride to see him in action.

It was natural that the day he set foot in Gisborne Geoff should join the Surf

Club, and natural that he should attend their dance. I saw him enter the ballroom, he saw me, and from then on no one else existed for either of us. We were both 18 years old.

Fortunately my parents loved Geoff as much as I did. Perhaps he was the son they never had. He and my Dad worked together in the garden, and often when they were hot — and sometimes when they weren't — they drank a glass or two of beer together. On Saturday mornings Geoff brought his car to our back lawn, where he took the motor to pieces and succeeded in putting it together again. I pleaded with him to make me a typewriter if there were any pieces left over, but there never were.

When we met I was doing various courses at night school, including accountancy, which Geoff was studying by correspondence. We had no notion that, in a world we felt was ours and where the sun always shone, a huge cloud hovered, waiting to change our lives for ever.

On the day war was declared, 3 September 1939, Geoff saw my prospective brother-in-law and others he knew join up — the red blood of Gisborne, they were dubbed. Too young to be accepted for the air force, which he yearned to be in, he wrote begging his parents' permission, stating his case and adding a postscript, 'Please say yes.' They could not resist the postscript and before long Geoff was one of what Governor-General Cyril Newall unwisely termed the 'gentlemen of the air force'. Training at Levin, he topped his course and was posted to England, co-pilot of a Wellington bomber.

In the meantime I had moved away from Gisborne to work. Kept alive by Geoff's letters I knew what he was doing, who he had met that we both knew, how he longed for the time when the war was over and we could be together again. He wrote:

Do you remember how the sea used to look at Wainui in the evening, with the moon shining over the point near Tatapouri? That's just how this sea looks, only the moon is redder and the whitecaps seem charged with a strange fire as they dance over the path of light thrown by the moon. Last night the sunset was one of the loveliest I have ever seen. The sun, huge and glowing, sank quietly behind a long bank of castellatus clouds. If you know what castellatus clouds are, you'll appreciate this. In case you don't, they have a flat base but look like castles in that they have towering battlements on their crest. The sun sank behind these clouds and lit all the towers with fiery red while the base was tinged pink, and the sky around was bathed in all the colours of a rainbow, blended together in the softest of shades. Strangely, there were shafts of green light in the sky, as though someone had turned on a green searchlight. Add to all this colour a pathway of gold across the shimmering sea and you'll have some idea of the beauty.

He wrote, too, of fellow-pilots who had been 'wiped out' and what a damned shame or a bad show it was. And of how New Zealanders over there 'get browned off in England when they can't see any blue sky for the haze and fog, especially when it's summer at home.'

Early in 1942 he was transferred to North Africa as part of the RAF's effort to prevent Rommel bringing in supplies. There was a long gap in mail both to and from him. On 23 February he wrote describing what he called his 'baptism of fire' over Benghazi which, he said, had a surprising amount of flak for such a small place.

On a raid last night I was so busy marvelling at the beauty of the tracer shells that I didn't have time to be scared. Tracers come up in all colours — red, green, blue, white, orange — and seem to float up ever so slowly, then, poof! A cloud of sparks and it's all over. Amazing, but deadly.

On 5 March 1942 Geoff was shot down in flames.

As always the first message said, 'Missing believed killed', but we all knew by this time what that meant. I went home to Gisborne.

Four days later (it was always four days) the telephone rang and my mother answered it. I heard her say, 'Oh!' and nothing else. Just 'Oh!' And I knew.

My father took the receiver, listened, and said, 'Thank you,' and put it down. Turning to me he said, 'A telegram from Geoff's father. Please tell Neva Geoff gone.'

I screamed and screamed and screamed, and a part of me is screaming still. My mother wept, and my father held me in his arms and said, 'We're here, Nugget. We're here.'

People came — neighbours, the minister, relatives, the postman. Few said anything but obviously wished they could. Some said, 'I know how you feel.' *Oh no you don't, oh no, you don't,* I said inside my head. But, 'Thank you,' I muttered. 'Would you like a cup of tea?'

'Time is a great healer,' others said, but it was another lie. Even if it was true,

I could not bear to hear it then and wanted to shout, 'Go away. Please go away.'

My parents offered no advice, no cliches. They were strong though and loving, often silent, but there. And my sister gave me her kitten.

Two days later I had a call from the Gisborne Drill Hall. 'We heard you were home,' a friend said. 'Would you come and help with the medical boards?'

Wearing dark glasses to hide my swollen eyes, I cycled to the drill hall next day. A week later, someone put a piece of paper in front of me and said, 'You have to sign this. You're in the army now.'

'Am I?' I said.

So that is how it happened, how I came to be in the army. It was quite unintentional. As I said, a mistake.

4

CHAPTER

A T THE DRILL hall I enjoyed being part of what was happening, though not for any reasons of patriotism other than hoping Hitler would be defeated. I enjoyed it because, like most young people, I was caught up with the excitement and adventure that consumed the men, that my sister's fiance felt, that Geoff felt, that all of our friends felt. No one I knew was against the war and I certainly wasn't. Not then.

I was sitting at my typewriter on my first day there when Howard the Scot walked in.

'Huh!' he said. 'Who said you could work in my room?'

'The Area Officer.'

'Huh!'

Howard was one of three civilians on the Gisborne Drill Hall staff. To me he was old, about 50. Tall and slim, he had little hair, and he peeked at you over his glasses in a slightly menacing way. He wore grey trousers, a white shirt, and a pale brown sports coat he never took off even on the hottest day. He was intolerant to the nth degree and he was a woman-hater. I considered him a challenge.

The other two civilians were as interesting. One was a man who had served in the First World War and had a wooden leg. He handled all telephone calls, and if anyone in individual offices did not answer his buzz he stood in his doorway and shouted for them, muttering not too softly, 'Where the hell has he gone?' or something worse. The other civilian was tiny, a beaver for work and genial and co-operative. Sadly, he imagined he was a comic, but all his jokes were old and repeated so often they were quite worn out. Whenever you asked him the time, he would look at his wrist and say, 'A quarter past a freckle,' or 'Half past a quarter to from.'

There were about a dozen uniformed staff. For some time I was the only girl, then three others came into my section and later a group arrived in Signals. I was put in charge of all the WAACs then and given three sergeant's stripes.

19

Howard the Scot and I worked hard. Each morning I was at the office by 7.30 and set things up for that day's medical boards in the large hall, carrying my typewriter out of the office on to one of the trestle tables. Then the recruits would arrive. For each I would put a form into my machine, ask the questions printed on it and type the replies. I knew many of the men and had to overcome my surprise at some of their answers. Many were farmers I'd danced with at woolshed functions and Hunt Club balls.

'Can you ride a horse?' was one question, an inappropriate one, I thought, in this war.

'No,' answered almost every farmer. I glanced up and smiled.

'Can you ride a motor cycle?' I asked then. And every time the answer was 'Yes'.

After his form was filled in, the prospective soldier went to another area of the hall to what was called the P and T department (P for Pee and T for tests such as blood pressure and heart), and before he departed altogether, he was sworn in on the Bible by our Area Officer. At least, he thought he was. But the captain often could not find his Bible, so he borrowed my old black Collins dictionary and, holding a thumb down the spine to conceal the title, performed the ritual.

Howard and I had two quirky running battles. Each Monday morning I brought a large bunch of flowers to work, put them in a vase on a shelf and waited. Howard would arrive, stand in the doorway, and sniff. 'Huh, more vegetables,' he would say, and I would smile at him. Also, when I arrived I always opened a window, and when he walked in a little later he would close it and smile at me. When he left the room I would open it a second time. At that, he left it open, and I smiled at him again. No word was spoken.

When he criticised women I didn't argue, because I'd been told his wife had left him. I imagined that as a result of this he was sour and resented my sharing his room simply because I was a female. Very aware that he was keeping a close eye on me, I was surprised one day as I sat typing away furiously when he stood behind me and said, 'You're not bad on that thing.' I knew I was accepted. From then on we verged on being friends.

Although I felt this something of an effort on Howard's part, he seemed genuinely sorry when he knew I was going overseas in the newly formed Clerical Division of the NZWAAC. As the day for my departure grew closer he appeared to try harder than usual to look miserable, but he certainly never volunteered any good wishes on our last day together at the office. Yet at the railway station with my parents and others next day there he was, Howard the Scot. Almost smiling, he shook my hand and said in his thick Scottish accent, 'For God's sake keep your sense of humour or you'll be sunk.'

NOW I'VE ARRIVED in Italy I am pleased I've had the drill hall experience, pleased to be familiar with army language, pleased I understand the sea of abbreviations used. Something like 'ETD AHQ rfts Adv Base is 2000 hrs 22 Nov. ADPS, 16 NZ LAD and 6 NZ Fd Coy to be advised' can not only be decoded, but makes sense. Just the same there will be plenty to learn. As we are welcomed almost literally with open arms by senior officers smothered in red braid, I wonder what it is they are equipped to teach us.

We are driven to Advanced Base where we have lunch in the officers' mess, tasting our first Italian *vino bianco*. Driving north towards Santo Spirito, we pass through Bari. It looks beautiful, although we are assured that it is not.

Thirteen kilometres north we arrive at the villa. I had imagined a fine residence in the country, surrounded by large lawns and spreading trees, the terrain sloping gently down to the sea where breakers roll lazily on to golden sand and the sun shines incessantly. But this is an ugly two-storeyed stone building whose frontage is edged by the footpath. The entire street of villas seems joined together, and even the trees lining it are sterile. They are oleanders, but not the oleanders with which we are familiar. These have slender trunks and their tops have been comicallly pruned to look like poodles' tails.

Siesta is over, and outside some of the villas dingily dressed men and women sit on kitchen chairs talking. From somewhere in the distance a voice sings 'O, Solo Mio', and a dog barks.

The five guards employed to protect us live in the downstairs portion of our large villa, with an entrance off the footpath. To the left of the building are grand iron gates which remind me of the opening of *Rebecca*. I can hear the voice of Wife Number Two, whose name you never know, opening the film with, 'Last night I dreamt I went to Manderley again. It seemed to me I stood by the iron gate leading to the drive, and for a while I could not enter for the way was barred to me.'

Our way is not barred to us. A guard unlocks the gate and we step onto the drive. Here we listen for our room allocations. Most of us will be upstairs in the main house, where a fine doorway off the drive leads into a marbled hall and thence to the stairs. Six others will occupy the Nissen hut erected especially for us at the rear of the large house. This is an oversized half-round barnlike metal structure.

Once again Nancy and I are bracketed. We are to share one of the three rooms into which the hut is divided. Our room, which opens on to the drive, is furnished with two beds complete with dark green mosquito nets, a tiny set of drawers, a narrow wardrobe and a kerosene tin of water. There is a small window and the floor is wooden. In each room there is a vase of flowers, put there by five kind Voluntary Aid girls from the Medical Division who work at the Convalescent Depot down the road and will live with us for a time.

Beyond our Nissen hut are six wide steps leading down to what was apparently once a large garden surrounded by a high brick wall, and close to the bottom of the steps is a two-holer latrine surrounded by scrim walls. Our kitchen and dining areas are in another house next door, with an entrance off our drive. As we settle in, the noise from the kitchen furnace almost drowns out the roar of the tanks on the road outside the gate and the hum of aircraft overhead.

After a large but tasteless dinner, Nan and I walk around the waterfront and then up behind the houses near our mess. Olive trees and grapes abound, St Joseph lilies bloom in profusion, and roses straggle along fences. On a tennis court four men play a strange game, either kicking a ball or hitting it with their heads. Wherever we walk the Italians say 'Hello Joe' and 'Just the job'.

In the morning we go to church in the main Headquarters administrative building where a Presbyterian padre makes us feel very welcome. We report to our offices tomorrow and will work seven days a week. Again Nancy and I have been placed together.

READY FOR WORK, we all meet in the large entrance hall of Headquarters and are escorted to our respective offices, Medical, Dental, 'A' (Administrative), 'Q' (Quartermaster), Military Secretary, Statistics, and so on. We are introduced to the Officer in Charge of Administration, commonly known as OICA. This is the big noise, our overall boss, Brigadier William George Stevens. He looks very stiff and very shy as he greets us en masse, and is pleased, I think, when this minor duty is over. I imagine we are meant to be in awe of these high-ranking officers, but having worked with them in Gisborne I see no reason to get excited about them. Already I know them to be as flawed as anyone else. Nancy disdains them on principle.

She and I will work for the military secretary, whose office is across the road from Headquarters in a candy-striped building which is rather pretty, set back amongst trees. The military secretary is important, we are told. He decides the fates of officers in the Division, whether they will be promoted, demoted, transferred, decorated and so on. He is so powerful, in fact, that he is known as God. In the circumstances, it seems logical to assume that Nan and I will be known as the angels in God's office.

5

*U*PSTAIRS IN THE candy-striped building the military secretary, Colonel Peter McGlashan, reigns, a dashing fellow who wears a black beret and walks and talks with supreme confidence. I am to do his work. Nancy will work for his deputy, and we will both do other work for the three men downstairs with us.

One of these, a sergeant-major, is very thin, very short and very nervy. He takes us on a tour of the office and when we reach the toilet he is overcome. We ask him what the problem is, and he can barely tell us.

'There is no key to the door,' he stutters.

We assure him that we have extremely high quality bladders, at which he twitches in a most satisfying way, and add that we are happy to walk around the corner to our mess if we wish to use a toilet. We think he is relieved (wrong word) to hear this.

'An only child, do you think?' I ask Nan.

'If he was ever a child he must have been awful,' she says.

'You only say that because he's short and you detest short men,' I laugh.

She does. Nancy loathes officers, and she loathes short men.

We have been here only two weeks and I am having trouble with this man. This morning there was an envelope on my typewriter with a sheet of blue paper inside it. Here is what the sergeant-major writes to Neva:

My darling Tiny, [where did he get that from? I'm much taller than he is. Is he comparing me with tall Nancy?]

I have been practically forced into this but I like it!

I'm a little non compus mentis if you get what I mean. If you don't, ask the rest of the camp. To come to the point, and believe you me, it's rather difficult — well, as I was saying,

1. Do you like me, because I like you?

2. Do you love me because I love you?

3. *Do you know that in three short weeks I'm going home?*
4. *Are you prepared to take a risk?*
5. *I'm still going home in three short weeks.*
6. *I'm all for it!*
7. *But not until I've someone to take home with me.*
8. *Would you come with me?*
9. *Please, darling.*
10. *An engagement?*
11. *I don't know, Neva, but you see, there isn't much time. Would you like your parents to know all about it first?*
12. *If you're agreeable to just cable them and go ahead, I can obtain an engagement ring from Egypt within a fortnight.*
13. *This is unlucky, so we'll pass on to . . .*
14. *And here again I just want to know if you really love me?*
15. *If you do, and perhaps doubt that I'm serious, what about coming out with me tomorrow night, just to wherever I'll take you?*
16. *I won't say any more — well, just because if you know how I feel you'll understand and I'll tell you everything tomorrow night.*
17. *Till then, darling, good night.*

The man is mad, I think. He must be. Or drunk. Or it's just a horrible joke on the part of the others at the sergeants' mess. I'm sure that's what it is, a joke. The bastards! But how embarrassing! What am I going to do? What is the sergeant-major going to do? I'll bet he wishes he could get the letter back.

I try to look blank as he passes my desk and I go on typing even when I see his feet stop alongside me.

'You got my note?'

'It's a silly joke, isn't it?' I say.

'I know I was under the weather, but I mean every word of it.'

'Don't be absurd. You don't know me.'

'Come for a walk now.'

We walk towards the harbour and this strange man convinces me that he means what he wrote. We argue and he says he is a serious person and that I am a hedonist and we return to the office. We are both furious.

I look up the word 'hedonist' in my dictionary.

I tell Nan about the letter. 'Do you think I'm a hedonist?' I ask her. 'Do you think pleasure is my chief aim in life? If you do, I'll kill you. And if you don't, on what do you think the sergeant-major bases his opinion?'

'He's crazy,' says this fount of all knowledge regarding short men. 'Take no notice of him.'

Easy for her, I think. I can't wait for the next few weeks to pass, but they do, with silent battle lines drawn. I feel bad though. I don't enjoy hurting the Sergeant-Major's feelings, even if it's his own fault, and I hope that when he gets home he'll find a girl just right for him. She won't be like me.

IN THE EVENINGS we girls sit around listening to the few records we have for the gramophone our friend left with us — some popular songs and a number of instrumental classicals, which are superb. We put a rug on the ground somewhere in the neglected garden, and anyone who likes can join us. Otherwise, all there is to do in the village is walk around the waterfront. It is so pretty, this wee fishing town, ragged but quaintly beautiful, the sort of place painters paint, though better to look at than smell. Boats ply to and from either the shore or the pier. We have already been swimming at the pier, surprising our menfolk when we arrived, as they were accustomed to bathing in the nude.

Everyone here is friendly. Yet on the buildings we see that 'Viva la Hitlers' have been replaced by 'Viva la Churchills'. And some of the girls who had bleached their hair for the Germans are now growing it back to its original black. They are very accommodating.

I try to imagine the war happening in Gisborne. How would I feel towards foreigners occupying buildings in my street, strutting about with confidence while we struggle with buckets of water because the retreating enemy has destroyed our supply, the soldiers well fed while we have no food supplies any more because our fields have been bombed? Even the birds have been eaten. I imagine we would say to ourselves:

Whatever country these soldiers are from, they can be our saviours at least temporarily if we behave properly, so of course we will be civil to them. It will be to our advantage, and we are not entirely stupid.

This is how it would be.

'Signorina beautiful,' says a girl passing with a young man. He asks, 'Possibile cigaretto?' No, they are no more stupid than we would be, poor as they are. And there is no doubt that they are poor.

Beyond the harbour the dirt road is edged by almost flat rocks. Walking in the long and lovely twilights, we smile at the families who are sitting on the footpaths talking and singing and laughing. The men play a finger game, their voices ringing out, 'uno' and 'quattro', 'tre' and 'due'.

Sometimes we leave the dirt road and sit on the rocks, looking out over the water. Unless there is a storm there are no waves here, just the serene Adriatic. But storms do occur, and when they do they arrive unannounced, catching fishermen at sea unawares. As the sky darkens boats scuttle into the harbour, by which time thunder is rolling and lightning stabs at the heavens with accusing fingers. The pier and the shore are suddenly pounded by clawing waves and there is shouting and a lot of waving of fishermen's arms as they fight their way to safety, watched by families who have run from their homes to stand fearfully on the shore.

From time to time, when men are down from the Division, some of us go into our Bari Club to a dance. For me it is exciting to find any man there who dances properly rather than walking around in time, or not in time, with the music. An Aucklander and I have discovered each other at these dances and we resent partnering anyone else in the room. Like Geoff, who never had a dancing lesson in his life, this man is filled with rhythm, his feet have a sense of adventure and he instinctively understands body language. So the two of us feel almost like one and I could dance for ever.

We are told we must go to the club to meet Mr Fraser, our Prime Minister, and play ladies over afternoon tea. You do not remind a Prime Minister that you have met him before if you are an insignificant WAAC. He was present at the posthumous VC Investiture for Second Lieutenant Te Moananui-a-kiwa Ngarimu. The ceremony took place on the East Coast, and some of us from the drill hall were there with our Maori Recruiting Officer — the one who farewelled his Ngatiporou boys when we were leaving Wellington. Governor-General Newall presented the medal to Ngarimu's father, Hamuera Ngarimu, who stood proudly in his dark suit. Slightly to his rear was his wife, Maraea, wearing a long black skirt and coat, and a black scarf over her head. Her feet were bare, and her expression achingly sad.

The lounge at the club is large, with potted palms spaced strategically here and there. We girls are in the minority amongst a lot of VIPs, with whom we mingle before afternoon tea. Walking around a palm I find myself facing the Prime Minister.

'Ah,' he says, 'and what are you doing over here?'

'I'm at administrative headquarters as a secretary, Mr Fraser.'

'How many words a minute do you write shorthand?' he asks.

I tell him, and he says, 'That's very good, isn't it?'

'What can I say?' I answer, and he smiles.

Not too long afterwards we meet again.

'And what are you doing over here?' he asks.

'I'm a secretary at administrative headquarters, Mr Fraser.'

'Ah, good!' he says. 'And how many words a minute can you write shorthand?'

I tell him.

'That's very, very good,' he says.

Just before we leave the function to return to Santo Spirito, he walks towards me and stops.

'What is your job over here?' he asks.

I tell him I work at administrative headquarters as a secretary and he says that is nice and how many words a minute do I write shorthand and I tell him and he says that is excellent isn't it and I agree.

I am pleased to learn later that he was not intoxicated, but virtually blind. No doubt he would prefer it to be the other way round.

A soldier at the Convalescent Depot asks me along there for supper because he has received a parcel of biscuits from home. For this I have late leave. Even so I have to persuade my friend to run home with me, and with one minute to spare we reach our mess exhausted. We needn't have bothered sprinting. No one had noticed that I had been out at all.

Now we are working six days a week instead of seven and, because it is obvious that we might do some hitch-hiking on our free day, we are lectured by a senior officer on possible dangers. We are warned about taking rides from Arabs and Poles in particular, but the officer adds that there is someone else to be wary of and that is our own young officer with a jeep.

Listening and watching, my eyes widen. I imagine the senior officer with a staff car, someone like himself, could be much more capable of being dangerous. I especially notice the way he keeps his eyes glued on our magnificent Minnie, who keeps her huge dark eyes glued on him.

THE MILITARY SECRETARY is just back from the Division. At the office we are dealing with reports on the battle at Orsogna where our troops were beaten back by a paratroop garrison before Christmas. We are sobered by the length of the casualty lists — more than 400 killed and more than a thousand wounded. Many survive, of course. Their bodies I mean. But what of minds?

A Maori sergeant has invited all of our staff to his mess after work to what he calls his 'forty-bloody-sixth' birthday. The atmosphere is a little cool and we find the resentment expected by Army Headquarters. It is men of this rank we are replacing, even competing with, and they don't like it. So we are calmly polite and pretend we do not notice their attitude. We talk to them about the war, of Orsogna and men we knew on the casualty lists, and say we thank God that it seems the war is close to being over and we'll all be back home soon. I think we succeed in not being hedonists. Were he here, our nerve-laden sergeant-major might acknowledge this, and certainly our host doesn't resent us or anyone else on this, his forty-bloody-sixth birthday.

Most days are simply full of work, but others are a mixture. Tomorrow Brigadier Stevens wants to take a pile of honours and award recommendations up to General Freyberg and it's urgent, with a capital U. I am almost cross-eyed typing. Mixed with this there is a stack of mail from home and a passionate note from the South African I met back in Cairo. Why can't men just be friendly?

Today my L.M. from the ship arrived at the office. He has come from Sicily and shows me two beautiful cloths he bought there. One is multi-coloured with a map of Sicily on it and the other is in various shades of blue, showing ancient figures and historical drawings. Each is in the finest cross-stitch, for which L.M. believes nuns are paid a penny a day. He gives me two small fluffy toy dogs from Naples. Or are they cats?

I show them to Colonel McGlashan, and he snorts. 'Bloody awful,' says he.

The men have decreed that we are forbidden to go out with Americans or we'll be knifed. Nan says she will go out with Americans if she wants to.

I go to my first opera and am over the moon. Two lovely Maori boys from Gisborne take me and I am almost sick with excitement. We see *Pagliacci* and *Cavalleria Rusticana*. The conductor of the orchestra has his five children with him there in Bari's Garrison Theatre and they come to our box to talk to us — Pepe, Radata, Sebina, Giovanni and Michaella. Aged between seven and 11, they are all quite beautiful. The theatre is huge, seating almost 3000, and the colossal domed ceiling depicts bullfights and biblical scenes, exquisitely executed. I am walking on a cloud.

A huge bundle of New Zealand mail has arrived, 19 letters for me. There are also four inter-unit letters from men in the Division who always reply immediately to my letters, so as far as they are concerned, I'm back where I started. There is also a passionate letter from the South African. In verse this time.

Nancy had an infected toe cut open today and fainted. Nancy fainting! She was feeling poorly later, and Maurine and Dorraine, who share the room next door, were a bit down because they didn't get any mail. So, feeling a shade guilty, I read them my poem from the South African to cheer them up.

Nancy has done what she said she would if she liked. She has been out with an American. We are glad she's back in one piece. But we noted an air of disappointment in her voice when she said it was hardly worth it because she wasn't threatened by any Kiwi.

Now I know why we see many Italians carrying dishes of food through the streets on their heads. It's because they cook in community ovens throughout the village. As they pass, their food smells delicious, much nicer than ours.

I tell lies. I am making a bathing suit out of a large cerise towel, and no one will take this as an excuse for not going to a dance or party, so I say I'm not very well. Then someone wants me to play badminton, for which I'd drop everything, and I can't, because if I go out I might see the person I've lied to. But there seems no alternative to lying. I don't want to exhaust myself being hedonistic. Often I like to be just me, alone with my thoughts, which are sometimes not suitable for sharing. I prefer to go to bed with a good book from the library. I brought four books from home, all small. One is a New Testament given me by dear old Mr Morris, who presents every soldier who leaves Gisborne with one; another is my Collins dictionary on which so many have been sworn into the army; the third is my old high school book of poems, *Palgrave's Golden Treasury*. The fourth is a book of crossword puzzles. These I do in pencil so I can erase my answers and start again.

6

CHAPTER

*T*HE OPENING OF the second front on Le Havre has called for celebrations throughout Headquarters. In an air of excitement we have listened to radio speeches by Eisenhower and Montgomery and Alexander, and read the good news in the *Union Jack* and our own *NZEF Times*.

Yesterday we all went to New Zealand's First General Hospital in Molfetta for yet another injection for typhus. I swear the doctor almost forgot to take the needle out of my arm and that he had kept his bluntest needle for me, but was encouraged to see a soldier faint as he waited in the queue.

MY L.M. HAS popped up again, to take me on a drive to Martina Franca to the south. (It's time I forgave him and called him George.)

We drive through Bari and then down the east coast to Monopoli where quaint water-wheels bestride the countryside. Mussolini's beautiful roads are tree-lined with profusely blooming oleanders, pines and loquats, every one severely trimmed. George claims that he can smell the rosemary hedges behind which olive plantations grow, but I don't believe him.

We turn inland towards Fasanto. From a height the white buildings of the town make it look as if giant wedding cakes have been parachuted into the thickly planted vineyards. We are in the midst of the 'trulli' country. The roofs of the trulli houses are shaped like an upside-down child's top, and are white. From there to the ground many houses are painted blue or green or yellow, with shutters of another colour again. Some domes have crosses painted on them, and some a letter, and on a handful of rooftops there are amusing weather vanes, one especially bringing a smile — a rooster wearing a top-hat.

And so to Martina Franca and through the ornate church, which is full of cherubs and columns and statues and priceless silver. As if we are the Pied Piper of Hamelin, we are surrounded on the footpath. Because Martina Franca is well off the main road and khaki is seldom seen here, people sweeping the street outside their houses stop sweeping, a girl mopping the side of a house as high as she can reach stops mopping, and a wizened old lady shakes us by the hand. She thinks we are Americans and explains that she has nine sons, eight of them living in California. The town is so clean compared with Santo Spirito, it might be in another country. As we prepare to leave two small girls emerge from a doorway. In their long white frocks heavily braided with lace and veils hanging to the ground, they walk hand in hand to confirmation.

WE HAVE A roster system at the mess. For a week we each supervise the work of our two Italian maids, Maria and Concetta, both about 18 years old. Maria is round and full of smiles, and seems always to be a little confused as she goes about her work. Concetta, who is tall and thin and erect, has a spiteful expression and rarely bothers to smile. She is very, very capable.

It is my week to do the supervising and I am almost afraid of Concetta, she is so disapproving of us all. This is Sunday and as she and Maria are Catholics they go to church before breakfast, so I set the tables for our meal and then rush upstairs in our main building to light the fire which heats our water. The fire is at the very top of the house, and I discover two things. Firstly that it goes out immediately, and secondly that when I finally get it to burn it needs stoking every 15 minutes.

Another duty is to take an inventory of everything in the mess, perhaps to check that nothing we have commandeered from the Italians goes missing. I do this, not forgetting to stoke the fire every 15 minutes, even rushing up to check it half way through the 15 minutes, to be on the safe side. When the maids are back from church, I am not entirely sure why it is not Maria or Concetta who is doing this — especially Concetta, who almost smiles as she watches me dashing up and down the stairs.

Our girls come from their offices for morning and afternoon tea, and at around 10 o'clock on my first morning on duty the cook gives me the usual baked beans to put into sandwiches. Baked beans! I give him my cigarette issue and he makes luscious tarts for afternoon tea. What a relief to get a message that the office is too busy to spare me for this mundane duty. A girl who is a smoker takes over from me tomorrow, so unless she can bribe the cook with something other than cigarettes we'll be back to baked beans. All next morning I take dictation and the military secretary tells me that his work, and therefore the work I do for him, is vital to the Division and that I must never do mess duty again.

I describe our water heating system and confess that I much prefer doing office work to being athletic at the villa.

'Good,' the colonel says.

'Speaking of water,' the corporal downstairs tells me, 'did you know that all the water at the Convalescent Depot has to be passed by the medical officer?'

'George,' I say, 'you're disgusting.'

When I finish transcribing my dictation I take the result upstairs. 'I don't enjoy some of this,' I say.

'What do you mean?'

'Typing adverse reports on officers you like isn't pleasant.'

'Being popular doesn't always make a chap a good soldier.'

I think of the gentle lieutenant on board ship who sat beneath the palm in silence. I tell Colonel McGlashan his name and ask, 'Do you know him?'

The colonel hands me a sheet of paper. 'Killed yesterday. A poor show.'

Does it have to be so simple? So clinical? A poor show? Is that what a man's life amounts to?

'He didn't deserve it,' I say. 'He was a lovely man. And his wife won't want to live now.'

'How do you know that?'

'He told me.'

'To you he revealed something as intimate as that?'

'Why not, if it's true?'

'You're a strange one, Neva Yvonne,' the colonel says.

7

CHAPTER

*F*OR THE LAST few days my eyes have been frantically itchy. I couldn't stop scratching them at a rooftop dance I went to with an American who works at our Convalescent Depot and is somehow in our Division. He is tall and thin, intelligent, ugly and possessive. I'm not sure that I like him.

The doctor isn't particularly interested in my itchy eyes. 'Conjunctivitis,' he says. 'It's the intense heat over here and the reflection off the white buildings. I suppose you wear dark glasses.'

'As seldom as possible,' I say.

'Why, you bloody fool?'

'I can't hear properly with them on.' I wait for a sceptical response.

'Not as unusual as you might think. All the senses dulled,' the doctor grunts, and sends me on my way with boracic powder and a bundle of cotton wool. Because it is easier than keeping my eyes open I go to bed at 7.30.

With my sore eyes, typing day after day is agony. Two of us now have the same itch, so together we go along to the hospital where a different doctor tells us we have a cold in our eyes. Armed this time with drops I feel happier, but days come and days go and the itch continues, making sleep hard to come by. Typing is an effort, writing letters is an effort, even concentrating is an effort. I try not to scratch my eyes out.

Today we wake at 3 a.m. to the sound of a German plane overhead. Three of us run out and stand in the dark by our latrine, watching the ack-ack. Geoff had written from Benghazi that had the ack-ack not been so terrifying it would have been beautiful, and watching now, I know what he meant. The sight is fearsome yet rivetingly beautiful, but though a shiver of awe goes down my spine I see no beauty, only Geoff. I don't think the others notice when I leave them standing in their nightdresses in the overgrown yard and go back to bed.

As if it was meant to be, next day Rod Taylor calls at the office, a friend of Geoff's and mine and one of the few Surf Club boys to have survived the war so far. A pilot, he is based at an RAF station north of us at Fóggia. It is very, very good to see him. He comes to dinner and amuses the girls with his charm and wit, and as he kisses me goodbye he doesn't mind my shedding a tear. I seem crammed full of tears at the moment.

The following day I am annoyed when a message arrives from the ugly American, criticising me for being with a man other than himself. I write a note explaining that my fiance had been killed and that Rod was a friend of us both, adding that I reserved the right to choose my own company.

The reply is more than I can understand.

I was in love with you from the first moment I saw you, I make no secret of it. Never for one moment did you owe me anything. I am not one of those fools who thinks worship puts a princess under an obligation. She is there to be adored. That is her metier. I was in love with you, not you with me. That is the beginning and end of the story.

But there is another side of the account. Every artist, author or composer knows his work depends on white-heat flame for successs. White-heat may be a high temperature or it may be ice-cold. Scientists say that if a thing is cold enough, it can burn with the same painful result as boiling point. The only real disaster is 98.4 degrees Fahrenheit, which is normal. There is nothing painful there. It is the temperature at which Brussels sprouts grow.

I will add that I was so bolstered by the hope that you would have married me; that I could have taken you back to California; that I could have introduced you to all my friends and been a very proud man; that I could have thrown everything into your lap. You and America add up to something.

On and on he writes.

'Hey, look at this,' I say to Nan. 'Isn't it queer?'

Nan reads the letter and laughs. 'You seem to attract peculiar men.'

'Perhaps that's because there are a lot of peculiar men about. Or maybe the war's making us all peculiar.'

I think of these two men, Rod and the American. One is kind and caring, understanding and undemanding, humorous and intelligent; the other is confusing and possessive, an unknown quantity, not a person I'd like to know in civilian life. His attitude towards me now, in the midst of a war, seems unforgivably petty.

Sitting in bed I pause in reading *Lady Into Fox* to consider the impact the war is having on all of our lives, and find it scary to consider what has yet to happen before it is over — further confusions perhaps, and possible sadnesses. Especially I think of Rod, who has three more raids to do before completing his second tour of operations. I hope to God he makes it. The world is much larger and much more tragic than the American's pain.

8

I'VE BEEN FRANTICALLY checking and typing copies of every citation for awards given since the war began. Fairness does not always seem involved. Some are given for comparatively simple acts and others for incredible bravery, often on behalf of the Gurkhas, many of whom have fought alongside our men. They are so strongly disciplined and fearless, they think nothing of laying down their lives for their friends. Is this brave or is it foolish? So much to wonder.

A rhinoceros beetle with an alarming wingspan and a long horn buzzed into our room last night as we were reading in bed and chose to land on my mosquito net. Nan and I emerged from beneath our nets and bravely killed it, placing the corpse on a ledge, with the intention of showing it to the other girls in the morning. But when we woke it was on a route march along Nan's tin trunk. We somehow managed to get him (we were sure it was a he) into our pail of water and put a cover on top. If he can swim, we don't know what to do next.

We now have siestas, working from 8.15 to 12.30 and from 4 to 6 p.m. During siesta we do what every mad Englishman would do. We go out in the midday sun. As we swim off the pier the Italians stay sensibly inside their *casas* sheltering from the intense heat.

Down from the Division and suffering from jaundice is Brian, a Gisbornite, who arrived from the Convalescent Depot on my day off with three bicycles and a friend. Dodging the thick military traffic, we pray every inch of the way as we pedal to the YWCA beach between here and Bari. We swim off and on all day and sail half way to Yugoslavia in a yellow rubber dinghy. Back at the Convalescent Depot we go to a Kiwi Concert Party show before I am escorted home 20 minutes late. To avoid being reported by the guards, with help I climb the brick wall at the rear of the mess. It isn't easy, but my aider and abetter, who will be at the Convalescent Depot for some time, assures me that he will bring along a sturdy box and put it by the wall to make further such exploits simpler.

We have had both military and civil police at the villa, as some clothing and towels are missing. Maria and Concetta are the suspects — in particular Concetta, who is such a grouse. Maria is far too pleasant to suspect.

Nan and I go north to the headquarters of an English artillery unit for dinner. We have a superb meal with New Zealand butter, which we don't get at our own mess. (What we get is English margarine.) The tablecloth is a sheet off someone's bed. In the twilight we swim at the unit's private beach where there is a raft, a jetty, and a strange craft. Wearing sandshoes, a straw hat and a scarf, an officer dog-paddles out to the raft and gives a superb diving display.

My aider and abetter plans to take me to the opera in Bari on my leave day. In the meantime he sends me notes rather than phoning. When I ask him why this is, he writes:

Back home I'm a great wool baron and if I had a phone in my castle I would never get any peace so, having done without the instrument for so long, I don't want to get involved with them now. Secondly (oh light of my eyes), I know how tired you would be after a day's hard work, and a note delivered into your fair hand saves you the trouble of walking to the phone. Everything seems OK for Thursday. I expect you'll be able to glamorise yourself at the club after being at the beach. (Hell, it's a long time till Thursday.) I'll call round for you about 1000 hours if that will suit you, and don't forget your leave pass. I think everything else is OK. Let me know if it isn't. Remember me to that terrible companion of yours.

Your exhausted B.

Things go wrong and another note arrives:

You must think me a bright sort of basket the way I try to arrange something and then put it off. The doctor confined me to bed for a few days and, as he has to put in a report to the military secretary on my health, I can't afford to put his back up, not even for your sake. Life has been exceeding dull lately and I'm just living for the next glimpse of you — it's the only thing that keeps me going. I hope I never have a day like last Thursday. How is your friend? I feel I should say something nice this time, but I can't. All my pleasant thoughts are for you, so you see how badly I've got it. I trust I will see you soon.

B.

PS

1. When's the boss coming home again?

2. I notice I really haven't apologised for mucking up your last leave day, and that's what this is meant to be about (so sorry).
3. Those eyes of yours (poor, poor wool baron).
4. For God's sake write and cheer me up.

A bit different from the American, thank heaven. I'll miss this zaniness when B. is posted.

Our troops are on the last hill overlooking Firenze, or Florence as we call it. In France the fighting is torrid, we hear, and the Germans coming to relieve front line troops are beaten with tiredness before their fighting begins, having marched 65–80 kilometres with 35-kilogram packs on their backs.

One of our English artillery friends has been down just to talk about the situation. He was in the Dunkirk mess, crossing from England three times in a yacht, stacking in 60 survivors in each trip. The French were unbelievable, he says, kicking other swimmers under the water in order to clamber into a rescue boat themselves. Once a body was under the water it wasn't seen again, everyone was so exhausted. Stretcher-cases were floated out — that is, if anyone could be found to do the job.

This officer gives me a copy of a German newspaper aimed at their own troops. It is called the *Frontpost*, and this issue is dated 12 January 1944. He translates sections for me. Under 'Brief News' one item reads, 'The area of British and American airfields in England is now 100,000 hectares.' Another reads, 'More than 43 percent of all Canadians between 19 and 43 are now armed.'

With the end of the war getting closer, there is much elation, which I share of course, but I find it impossible not to think of all the lives already lost and others still to be lost — for what purpose, God knows. I can't believe there is any plan dictated by Him for what is happening, all the killing and devastation by the enemy and ourselves. And God wouldn't be so silly as to take sides, would he? Isn't mankind just that to Him rather than Germans or Russians or French or English or anything else? Something is very wrong and I am somehow hurt inside at the elation I see.

But wait, I tell myself. Elation is to be expected. Why the hell shouldn't those who have survived let their hair down, why shouldn't they get thoroughly drunk and make idiots of themselves? In such circumstances, drinking and laughing and being absurd can be very close to crying with relief. There is much for which to be grateful but much pain too in remembering mates that have gone, old mates and men who had become mates overnight, mates who had shared unspeakable sights and unspeakable thoughts. Inside many men there must be a huge lake of unshed tears. Inside me there is a puddle. I must be tolerant.

The girls of course have not the same reasons for such elation, and inwardly I know that at times I am judgemental when I see some enjoying themselves seemingly too much. I am constantly aware of the gap Geoff has left in my life and I suppose I am a bit crabby underneath. Or hypercritical. But I won't let anyone know. I'm far too cunning for that. Besides which, much of the time I, too, am enjoying myself. But there is a fine line beyond which I can not let myself go.

After considering these things I am enormously pleased when Sid the Provost puts his head inside our door. 'How about a beer?'

'Great,' I say.

9

CHAPTER

*O*UR MESS IS a mess. The four-year-old sister of our Concetta has died so she is not at work, and Maria is away ill. With a mix-and-match arrangement we are managing, but in the midst of it all Maria arrives crying with pain. She can not stand it, she must see a doctor, she doesn't know what to do, her family doesn't know what to do, can I tell her what to do? I have no idea what to tell her to do, but obviously someone must do something.

I take her to our army doctor who examines the dreadful abscess on her left breast. He orders hot packs and aspirins throughout the day. By the morning poor Maria is desperate and begs me to kill her, the pain is so intense. I take her back to the doctor who orders me to get an ambulance and take her into the civilian hospital in Bari. The ambulance people won't take Maria because she is not a military personage and King's Regulation such-and-such forbids the carrying of civilians in War Department transport.

I telephone Sid the Provost. 'Sid the Provost, is that you?'

'Can't you just call me Sid?'

'No, Sid the Provost. Listen, Maria is ill and we must get her into Bari to the civilian hospital. Can you get a vehicle?' He will, I know, because Sid the Provost likes to feel important. He is short and thin, and I doubt that anyone has ever made him feel needed.

'Regulations say no civilians in . . .'

'In War Department transport. The ambulance guys told me. I'll start again. Sid the Provost, can you somehow get a vehicle?'

'Sure,' he says.

'You're wonderful,' I say. 'Can you come now?'

He can not possibly admit that he can come now. His status dictates otherwise, will not allow him to bow to the wishes of another human being. Well, not immediately. The matter needs a little thought.

'I'll do my best,' he says. Within minutes he is at the gate with a five-ton truck.

Maria and I pile in beside him and he drives like a fiend into Bari, where we get totally lost. When anyone gives instructions Sid the Provost ignores them, because he considers himself a decision-maker, but after almost two hours of finding ourselves in blind alleys and becoming entangled with loading and unloading trucks, he accepts defeat and obeys directions given by a pretty signorina. In pain, Maria is weeping torrents of tears.

When we find ourselves at the front entrance of an *ospedale militare* rather than *borghese*, Sid the Provost shouts, 'Christ, where is the bloody civilian hospital?'

Just as he appears ready to step down from the truck and leave it to Maria and myself, a small boy who has been listening while gazing at us with huge brown eyes and lashes absurdly long says in pidgin English, 'I take you to the other hospital.' As he speaks he pulls himself up into the truck, squeezes in beside us all and closes the door.

With the aid of much arm waving he finally says, 'Hi, Joe, turn right,' and we are there.

For his trouble he asks for a box of matches, which Sid the Provost is about to refuse.

I open my eyes wide and say, 'Sid the Provost, don't be such a bastard.' A box of matches changes hands and the boy disappears.

Maria and I pass through two courtyards to reach a door where a very dirty man examines the army medical officer's note of admission and says, 'No capisco.' He doesn't understand? What now? Ignoring the man's angry voice, we walk on quickly to find ourselves in a large, unclean hall where we are confronted by another dirty man wearing only pyjama pants and a cap. He does not understand the note either, or says he doesn't, and takes us to a kitchen where a nun is shelling boiled eggs. It is a relief when she and Maria get to the matter in hand, that she and I are there because Maria must be admitted to hospital and have her abscess treated.

But Maria turns to me in tears. It is impossible, she says. There are no beds. She must go home. The nun shouts this to me in her rapid Italian, which I feel it wise not to understand. I wave the doctor's note and in my rapid English insist that a *dottore* look at Maria's abscess. Maria translates this, and turns again to me. The nun is a *dottore*.

Oh, my God! 'Get a *maschio* doctor, a male doctor, a man doctor.' I shout and wave my arms because this seems necessary. The nun glares with disapproval and leads us to a hallway where a man I hope is a doctor examines Maria's abscess. I am pleased to see him register concern.

'A bed,' I say with as much authority as I can muster. 'A *letto*.'

The doctor looks almost timid and agrees that there is, indeed, exactly one bed available.

I tell Maria that I will telephone the hospital each day and, when the time is right, will come and collect her, totally relying on Sid the Provost's co-operation as I make this promise.

Maria is upset. She wants me to stay, but I hug her on her right side, well away from the abscess, and vanish lest the doctor decides there is no bed available after all. As I leave he asks if I am English or German and when I point to my shoulder tabs which spell out 'New Zealand' he tells me he did not know the Dutch were fighting in his country.

Sid the Provost pretends to be furious that I have taken so long to have Maria admitted to the *ospedale borghese*, but is soon full of smiles at the success of our expedition and says 'We did a good job, didn't we?' He buys me a cup of tea at the club before driving maniacally back to Santo Spirito.

10
CHAPTER

A HUGE PILE of New Zealand mail today, thank goodness. Nine letters for me, plus a parcel from Mum, oh bliss! I know about getting parcels ready for posting overseas. Buy the tin from a tinsmith, fill it with your goodies, return it to the tinsmith to seal, take it home and address it with black bicycle enamel. Sew it up strongly in sacking, address a cotton label and stitch that to the sacking. Then carry the parcel to the post office and send it off. What a business! Thank you, Mum.

The excitement is intense as I unstitch and cut and lever, and while others watch I feel like a Cheshire cat. Inside is a batch of Mum's famous Afghans and a tin of talcum powder which has burst and sprinkled itself all over the biscuits. I will never tell. We dust the biscuits off, light the primus, open a tin of coffee and milk and have what we call a party under a tree in the long grass beyond the scrim toilet, with the gramophone wound up and playing gentle Bach music.

Every day I feel I have never worked so hard and I am so, so tired. I wish there was some way you could make six copies of almost everything you type without the dirty carbon paper and having to bash so firmly on the keys to make sure that copy number six is as legible as copies numbers five, four, three, two and one. Copies go to Wellington or London and Egypt, where they are delivered to unit commanders and admin records, pay offices, quartermasters, et cetera; so as well as typing hard you have to keep your wits about you. When the colonel returns from the Division he dictates to me for days and then I sit at my machine pounding until I feel cross-eyed, seldom looking up because I like to finish a job as quickly as possible. If I was paid by the hour I'd be a pauper. If I was paid by the page I'd be a millionaire.

Pressure of work means I am really far too tired to walk around the waterfront with Mac, an RAF pilot — but I do. He partnered me when we went to a dance at his unit recently, and in return for such civility we always invite our partners to our mess for a meal. Mac is a softly spoken Scot, with gentle manners. As we walk companionably he speaks of raids he has been on, of the rear gunners' plight, then of more personal things. He tells me about the small town he lives in back home, his sister and brothers, and his father's job at a school and what the family does at weekends and his mother's roast pheasant and how beautiful the sea is tonight, and the moon, and would I like to walk out to the edge of the rocks. And I say yes, oh yes, that would be lovely.

So we sit and I listen, and I tell of my mother's Afghans and talcum powder and my farmer father and the sports my sister and I are involved in and how we wash our hair on Saturday mornings and take care of our cuticles and do out our rooms and with our tennis racquets walk up and down the cabbage rows killing white butterflies and sing around the piano and dance and dance in town and in woolsheds and in country halls and sometimes drink a little too much of Gisborne's Gold Top ale. Meanwhile the sea lazily laps against the rocks at our feet and the friendly moon smiles down on us in the fast fading light.

Mac glances back towards the road. 'I think there's trouble. We'd better go,' he says. His tone is urgent.

We stand up and turn. On the road to our left is a soldier, directly in front of us is a soldier, and to the right is a third soldier. As we walk across the flat rocks to the road the three men close in around us. There is no way we can pass them. We are trapped. And the beautiful twilight is suddenly ugly and fraught with fear.

The soldiers have swarthy evil faces, and all three are looking at me. The tallest, the leader, holds a knife at Mac's chest and in broken and crude English puts their plan to him. Each will rape me, and then he, Mac, can do the same. My heart will jump right out, I am sure, it is thumping so hard, and my mind refuses to work. As the man speaks a large cloud pulls a curtain across the sky and the night deepens dramatically and eerily.

Does Mac think before he acts, I wonder? Much shorter than the knife-holder, he punches the soldier in the face, at which one of the others picks me up, throws me over his shoulder and runs into a ploughed field, a second man running alongside. My shouts of 'Help, English, help,' are stifled by the second man putting a hand over my mouth. Well into the field the man carrying me drops me roughly to the ground, then both men begin pulling and tearing at my clothes as I lash with my arms and kick and squirm. My tie and blouse are taken off, and my shoes and slacks, and I wish to God Mac was here to help. But he is lying on the road stabbed, I am sure. Dead perhaps.

The silhouette of the man with the knife suddenly appears. For a moment he stands speaking in an urgent tone, but what he is saying I can not understand. With renewed energy the men drag off my suspender belt and stockings. All I am wearing now is a sanitary belt and a bulky sanitary towel, but while this puzzles the soldiers, it does not deter them.

One man has taken off his trousers, a second holds my legs apart as I kick and struggle, and the man with the knife kneels at my head holding its tip on my forehead while with his free vicelike hand he grips one of my arms.

The trouserless man is crouching on top of me. His penis is large and hard, and he is obviously very angry as he prods it to left and right of my sanitary pad.

There is a lot of muttering in a strange language as I fight on. I feel certain I am going to be killed but I'd die fighting, bugger them, so although I am tiring I summon up energy that isn't there. I am too furious to be afraid.

After what seems a very long time a row of torchlights appears over a rock wall some distance away. 'Here, here, here,' I shout. I can not shout enough.

The three soldiers run off into the darkness, but one returns, grovelling by my head as I am about to stand up. Thinking he must be feeling for his knife, I hold him by the ankle, but he is too strong and easily pulls away. The torchlights follow the silhouettes of the three men. Soon I vaguely see and hear Mac at my side. 'I'll go after them too,' he says breathlessly.

'Please stay,' I say. 'Please.' Getting to my feet in front of him wearing nothing but my sanitary towel, I don't care if he is the entire Royal Air Force as with fumbling fingers I find my bits and pieces of clothing and put them on — all but my shoes and stockings, which I hold in my hands. I am shivering now. I have no idea whether or not Mac watches me getting dressed, but I suspect that he doesn't.

For a moment he puts an arm around me, apologising for what has happened, as if he is responsible. He explains that after punching the soldier with the knife, he ran to a nearby camp where a team was organised to come to my rescue.

Unable to catch the soldiers, the torch-bearers take us to their headquarters, where we are plied with cups of hot syrupy-sweet tea. After my last half hour, this is sheer ambrosia.

'The men involved in this are Palestinian Arabs attached to my unit,' the commandant says. 'We've checked and the three who are missing are particularly bad.' He makes a note of Mac's name and rank and unit, and of mine, and tells me I am lucky to be alive. He is an earnest man of around 50 who would, even in happier circumstances, have found it difficult to smile.

A young lieutenant accompanies us to our units — Mac to his, I to mine. His presence is comforting, especially as the driver of the car is another Arab, not the sort of person I most want to be near.

At the gate of our mess Mac kisses me briefly. 'I can't tell you how sorry I am.'

I say it wasn't his fault, that it had been bad for both of us, and that he had been pretty courageous, might even have saved my life. 'So thanks, Mac,' I say. I am very close to tears.

I am pleased when the guard unlocks the gate and I am walking down the wide familiar driveway and can see a light shining from the room Nan and I share in the Nissen hut.

From where she is reading under her mosquito net, Nan asks, 'Have a nice time?'

'If you put your book down I'll tell you.'

Nan is fine. As fine as anyone can be, anyone who can do nothing but listen. Poor Nan! After expressing her thoughts colourfully, she suggests I get into bed and try to sleep. You see, she is fine. What else can she do?

I DON'T SLEEP. In the morning, I go to work. I want to work hard, to stop thinking of last night.

Why I am surprised when Sid the Provost walks into the office with the commandant from the English camp I don't know. It hadn't occurred to me that the unit to which the Palestinian Arabs are attached would undertake an investigation. In retrospect, I suppose I am suffering from shock.

Our own WAAC officer arrives too, and our 'A' Branch colonel. There will be an identification parade, I am told, and, if Mac and I are able to recognise anyone, there will follow a summary of evidence and a court-martial. The commandant of the Palestinian Arabs' camp says this is a most serious case, as I am in the British forces and not simply any little local girl.

Oh, I think, what a pompous remark — as if one girl is somehow more worthy than another. But there is always something peculiar about a man who finds it hard to smile, I tell myself. Although I need this particular one, it isn't compulsory to like him.

Our 'A' Branch colonel says, 'They tell me you were very brave.'

'I was too angry to be brave.'

The WAAC officer describes me as being a particularly calm person, and the colonel suggests I take time off work. Time to get over it is the way he expresses it. He doesn't understand of course. Doesn't understand the violation, the horror, the desperation, the fear. How can he, a man? For me the memory will not go away by taking a day or two off work.

There is another thing no one will understand. That having coped with Geoff's death I can cope with most things. My way is always by working and working and working. It will not help me to stay in our Nissen hut, thinking about the Palestinian Arabs. I will try to put them in a closed compartment of my mind for as much of the time as possible and concentrate on work. Then the horror will fade away.

This is what I think. I am wrong of course. Sometimes it is bearable, then unexpectedly out of the closed compartment comes that penis, and I feel its strength as it pokes and prods, hear the annoyed voices of the Palestinians, am aware of the tip of the knife on my forehead, feel the man pull his leg from my hands as I try to hold him. But always it is the penis. Its smoothness and strength.

The day following the episode the lieutenant from the English unit arrives at the office. 'We've been over the field,' he says, 'and we found a cap with a name in it. Akad.' For a moment he hesitates. 'Perhaps I shouldn't tell you this. In Egypt this fellow came up on a murder charge, but unfortunately it couldn't be proved. You're a very lucky young lady.' Unlike his commander, this man can smile easily, and does now, a soft, kind smile.

I swallow and say, 'I feel lucky.'

'It's going to be tough for you but we'll make it as easy as we can, Miss Morrison.'

Wishing he was much older than he is, around my own age, I assume that back at his unit he and others have discussed my nakedness, perhaps laughed about it. And they'll have spoken, too, about my sanitary towel. The embarrassment! I wish myself almost anywhere but where I am.

'You'll be seeing a lot of me before this is over, so you'd better call me Cliff,' the lieutenant says.

'You'd better call me Neva.'

11
CHAPTER

*T*HERE IS SOME concern. We are about to move north to Senigállia and it is thought that I might have to stay behind and live in the club in Bari until the court-martial is over. Because I dread the prospect of living with strangers, I plead with everyone to prevent this happening if they can, and they have been supportive. They feel sorry for me, I think, especially the pleasant lieutenant. Somehow the parade date has been moved forward, and I might not be separated from the other girls after all.

Mac and I are summoned to the English unit. Twelve men are lined up in two rows of six, and every one of them looks evil. Walking along the rows and reaching Akad, I recognise him. His eyes are huge with fear, and I feel fear myself looking at them. The men are rearranged and Mac walks along the rows. He, too, identifies Akad.

Sid the Provost drives me to and from the parade in stony silence. He is consumed with anger because he heard of a New Zealand girl's plight through an English unit. But now he is filled with importance because he has been made responsible for getting a lengthy statement from me for use in the forthcoming summary of evidence and court-martial. His mana is high.

Someone else has been upset. The colonel of our 'A' Branch sends me a message saying he hasn't slept properly since my Palestinian Arab experience. He hasn't slept!

I tell Nan. 'Poor Colonel,' I say derisively.

Nan looks at me sternly. 'Neither have I,' says she.

After finishing his report, Sid the Provost is looking very self-satisfied. We've gone over it seemingly endlessly as he feels I might forget some points at the summary of evidence and the court-martial, as if that were possible, there or anywhere else. Sid, you have no imagination whatever, you are just a dolt. Just the same, we swim together off the pier afterwards and laugh when we are swept into a hole. I have no notion why we laugh.

My things had been taken into the Bari Club, but now the colonel from 'Q' is picking me up to collect them as I will definitely be moving north with the others. He tells me that the communication signals from the north were too faint to hear when he tried to get a decision about me.

I am not certain that I believe the audibility bit. 'How faint were the signals?' I ask.

'Very,' the colonel answers, and his lips move as mischievously as any senior officer's will allow themselves.

People are very kind. My boss, Colonel Robert Peter Reid McGlashan, the military secretary, writes to me in a hand only barely decipherable but to which I have become accustomed. Nevertheless it is as full of character as the man himself, and I quite enjoy the guesswork necessary as I hold a sheet of his writing in front of me. It's rather like doing a cryptic crossword puzzle.

This is what I am almost certain the colonel writes when it is thought I will have to stay in Bari.

Dear Miss Morrison,
On my return from Div yesterday I heard about your very nasty experience. I'm very sorry such a thing should have happened. I also hear that it was thanks to your clear headedness and courage that they have managed to get one of the men responsible, which is a very good show indeed.

Such a nuisance for you that you might have to stay on for the trial, etc. If so, we hope to see you back safe and sound, and none the worse for a very sticky experience.
Yours sincerely,
Peter McGlashan.

'Thoughtful of him to write, wasn't it, Nan? But perhaps he could have chosen a better word than "sticky".'

Nan mutters about colonels, and I wonder how long she will continue to be so disparaging about officers, even junior ones. Her attitude is an enigma to us all.

All morning I have been at the English Special Investigation Branch being grilled by a captain and also by a Yugoslav girl who is a lawyer and a captain in Intelligence. I feel drained when it all ends — I am a nothing, I almost don't matter. Indisputable facts are what they are interested in, of course. They do not mean to be steamrollers.

It is after two o'clock when Cliff, the lieutenant, takes me back to the office. To me he represents stability in this messy business, and I am absurdly grateful for his presence.

So I tell him, 'You're important to me right now.'

'That's fine with me,' he says.

We leave for Senigállia on Monday. The hour, the minute can't come soon enough. Much as I have loved little Santo Spirito and my introduction to the sad war-torn south of Italy, I can't wait to shake the place off my heels.

12
CHAPTER

*T*HE AIR IS autumnal. I look out from the scrim two-holer at the branches of the leafless fruit trees reaching up to the weak sun. Their orange leaves have fallen amongst the weeds and make a pretty speckled carpet which will be messy to walk through when I come home late and climb over the back wall. Already the tomato field on the other side is a bog, so that when you take your shoes and stockings off the mud squelches between your toes.

When we leave here, I will think of this place often and, despite the last couple of weeks, with a good deal of affection. Because, Santo Spirito, you introduced me to the unforgettable Italy with its special smells and sights and people — the heat rising from the roadways, the once-lovely homes we have taken over for our headquarters, the large iron gates and shrub-edged driveways, the moody sea, the humour of the fishermen, the 'O Solo Mios' wafting in the twilight outside the poor yet rich villas, the Italianness of it all. I will be sad to leave you, Santo Spirito, but glad to leave you.

Just after 4 a.m. the six of us in the Nissen hut take our beds to pieces. Nan and I wash in five centimetres of rusty water and go to breakfast, which consists of a cup of tea and a long, cold sausage roll made yesterday. Barely palatable, it clings to the teeth as if in fear of something worse than being swallowed.

By 5.30 a.m. we are on the road, Maurine and I in the back seat of a car and very comfortable. It is still quite dark. As dawn breaks low blousy clouds billow like smoke, the sky above them streaked with long grey ribbons. Geoff would have described them otherwise. A pilot.

The wee villages we pass through have been bombed until only shells of buildings remain, or simply rubble, yet here and there owners are searching amongst the debris for something recognisable. Just north of Fóggia we stop for a roadside cup of tea, and as we stand in the sunlight on this still yellow day I watch an old lady in a long grey frock, wisps of hair hanging from a black headscarf, as she bends and pokes, bends and pokes, then turns to face us. In her hands she holds a bright blue chamber-pot.

Nestling in the foothills south of Cassino is a small town in which the Germans are said to have herded women and children into a cave, then filled the cave in. Can this be true? It is true. On the edge of the out-of-bounds town of Cassino white crosses denote the graves of 18 Germans; each one is marked 'Unknown German Soldier'. Close by are 50 New Zealanders' graves, a tin hat placed on each, and a name. One is of a member of Geoff's Waikanae Surf Club. A vision of his tall athletic figure springs to my mind, and I see him swimming out strongly through the breakers. I see his father, too, walking to work as he does each day, swinging the only arm he has after serving in the First World War.

What desolation all around — the monastery a wreck, the wired-off ground full of shell-holes and mines, every home destroyed. Each is a monument to bravery certainly, but also to futility, even madness. Although many have already been removed, the wrecks of Allied and German tanks, trucks and planes lie abandoned. Signs point down side roads. 'War Cemetery' they say. Then we pass Million Dollar Hill, which cost the Americans an appalling number of lives. Maurine and I look at each other and shake our heads. Does she feel as I do, sad and angry and uncomprehending? I can not ask her because I can not speak. Maurine does not speak either.

On and up the winding road to pretty little hilltop Ferentino, badly damaged, but picturesque still, its buildings clean and painted white or a faint pink or orange, and softened by the greenness of trees.

Then Rome! We expect a grand entrance, not a route through a railway area and back streets. But we are quick to forgive. How can you not forgive a city as overwhelmingly beautiful as Rome? For three nights we will be staying at our New Zealand Club, once the grand Quirinale Hotel, before carrying on to Senigállia where we will be stationed — for how long we don't know. As our Division moves north, so do we in our 2 NZEF Administrative Headquarters.

APART FROM BEDS, the room Maurine and I share in Rome has a table, bedside bookcases with books actually in them, a sizeable wardrobe and a hand-basin each. The curtains draw back and the sunblind draws up. When we discover these last two facts we sit on our beds and laugh and laugh, because this is all so different from our Nissen hut. I think our laughter has something to do with

Cassino too. I think it is an outlet for our emotions, a relief. But not all of it. We are 24 years old and ready for laughter. When possible, that is.

The Welfare girls at the club warn us that prices in Rome have escalated by 300 percent and that we can blame the Americans, who are here in their thousands. When asked how much, *quanto costa*, vendors now reply in dollars.

In the evening a crowd of us dance at the Nirvanetta Club to the strains of a heavenly Italian orchestra. I foxtrot with what we think is a Pole, who appears before me, clicks his heels and says 'Iss okay?' as he points to the dance-floor. He smells very pleasant, has perfect rhythm, and at the end of each dance clicks his heels anew and waits for the music to strike up again. When our spell together is over, he smiles and says, 'Grazie,' so perhaps he is Italian after all. With a final clicking of heels he is gone.

A number of times I dance with an officer I have not met before. Jock wears a kilt and does a fascinating little jump at corners. One of the things I like about him is the fact that he requests Strauss waltzes, so wonderful to dance to, but I do not think of him as being exactly memorable, just extremely nice.

When we gather as a tourist party with a guide the following morning, there is Jock. He is by my side for the rest of the day. Together we admire St Peter's and listen in awe as voting for a new Pope is described. Black smoke issuing from a chapel chimney turns to white as wet straw is replaced with dry. We admire paintings and columns and frescoes and statues and marble and alabaster; we agree that the Victor Emmanuel monument looks like a giant wedding cake, and later think we prefer St Paul's to St Peter's because it is . . . well . . . smaller, less ostentatious.

Our four Catholic girls are soaking up their visit to Rome avidly and are having their rosary beads blessed by the Pope.

Lovely flirtatious Minerva sees things differently from these four. When viewing a priceless piece of jewellery gifted to the church she almost swoons and says, 'Oh, how exquisite that would be on a plain black frock.' She looks at the priest who is accompanying us and sighs. 'Wonderful,' she breathes. Does she mean the jewellery we ask one another, or the blushing priest?

Another thing that puzzles us is that despite the rules we have about dress Min always manages to be wearing something different from the rest of us. Who gave her the white duffle coat for instance, and where did she get her nylons while we others still wear ugly khaki stockings? To date she has not been reprimanded by any of the colonels. From the way they look at her, we even wonder if this is where these things have come from. With a well-bred but slightly audacious air she walks like music amongst us, perfectly aware of an audience. But she reveals nothing. She is as silent on the matter as a sphinx. We are not jealous or criticial of our Min though, because she is as kind as she is beautiful. We simply accept that physically speaking we are inferior beings, and we watch with interest as she gathers about her a group of admirers who could represent the League of Nations. But where will it all end, that is the question?

As I think of Min I am reminded of my parents. Be careful not to flirt too much, they would say. Be careful — he is a Catholic; be careful not to . . . or where might it all end? Especially my father, so protective of his daughters, alarmed if he saw me riding home from school on my bicycle with a boy who lived around the corner from us.

'Be careful, Nugget,' he said more than once. 'Riding home with boys you could finish up like Joan Byron.' Joan Byron was the prettiest girl in my class and she rode home with a different boy every day of the week; and, vivid green with envy, I used to think, if only I could. If only, instead of being wimpishly shy, I could actually be like Joan Byron. Finish up like her.

By now, of course, in these Italian days, I have given up being shy, and Jock does not make me feel that way. He is too down-to-earth, too stoical, too Scottish.

'I was here years ago,' he says, 'and I'm taking you somewhere special — that is, if you're interested — to the Protestant cemetery to see the graves of Keats and Shelley. Would you like that?'

'It would be a breath of fresh air.'

Jock points to the beech trees above John Keats' grave. 'Planted by English residents of Rome who knew they were Keats' favourite.'

Carefully I pick six leaves to preserve for myself and friends, then solemnly Jock and I read the famous inscription on the tombstone below:

This grave contains all that was mortal of a young English poet, who, on his deathbed, in the bitterness of his heart at the malicious power of his enemies, desired these words to be engraved on his tombstone — 'Here lies one whose name was writ in water.'

We examine the grave of Keats' artist friend, buried alongside him. 'Look on the back of the stone,' Jock says. There I read the names of those in Rome who paid to have the friend's heart brought from England to be buried here.

And although Keats wished that his name be omitted from his grave, on a nearby wall his name is spelled out in the first letter of each line of a short poem:

Keats, if thy cherished name be 'writ in water'
Each drop has fallen from some mourner's cheek,
A sacred tribute such as heroes seek
Though oft in vain for deeds of valour.
Sleep on, not honoured less for epitaph so weak.

We can not leave the cemetery without sparing a thought for Percy Bysshe Shelley, drowned near Genoa at the age of 27. His great friend is buried beside him, Edward Trelawny, on whose tombstone is this verse:

These are two friends whose lives were undivided;
So let their memory be now they have glided.
In the grave let not their bones be parted,
For their two hearts in life were single-hearted.

Rather sadly we leave the cemetery. 'You'll never know what being here means to me,' I tell Jock. Indicating my throat, I add, 'I'm full right up to here with emotion.'

'I know. I was watching your face. Did you know you have eyes that speak?'

I laugh. 'If it's true, I hate to think what they might be saying sometimes.' I'll check in the mirror just the same. See if he was right.

Visiting the Saint Sebastian catacombs where Christians hid from the pagans should be a solemn occasion, but somehow we girls are overcome by mirth. It is the fault of the accoustics. We are led by a monk carrying a long stick with a candle on the end, and we all carry lighted candles which have cost us 10 lire apiece. The monk waves his candle towards niches in the walls or at vaults, and says in a sepulchral tone, 'More bones.'

Walking one behind the other, each of us relays 'More bones' over a shoulder, and as the words are repeated, they become elongated. 'Mooooore booooones,' we drone, our voices mingling and echoing and surging through the tunnels. 'Moooooore boooooones.' Even our Roman Catholic girls can not be serious.

One last evening in Rome. Jock takes me to the British Officers' Club for dinner and then to the Nirvanetta. He tells me he lives in England, not Scotland, which surprises me.

'Why are you in the Queen's Own Cameron Highlanders then?'

'Because my father was.'

'So he was born in Scotland then?'

'No,' Jock says, 'but his father was in the Queen's Own Cameron Highlanders, you see.'

'No, not at all.'

'Don't worry about it,' Jock says. So I don't. He is very nice, and I am extremely fond of the kilt. This has been a pleasant interlude.

DRIVING NORTH NEXT day we discover an Italy far more beautiful than in the south. Cultivated fields create a patchwork of colours, although the earth is pockmarked with bomb-holes. We cross many Bailey bridges; some are triple double, others double double, depending on how many widths of steel provide their diameter and how many decks each has. And atop each hill is a small town with church spires and towers reaching for heaven, and trees and pastel-coloured buildings, and a wall apparently preventing the town from tumbling down the steep slope.

Almost nine hours after leaving Rome we arrive in Senigállia where we girls are taken to two adjacent very lovely houses, our quarters. Despite the wide streets and the fine homes, there is a feeling of desolation here. The railway line parallel with the beach is twisted drunkenly, little remains of the hospital, and even the trees look tired.

We are 13 kilometres behind the front line and will adhere to strict blackouts. On the houses we live in there are shutters which must be closed at dusk. There is no water, nor any electricity. A generator is being organised, but for a time we will carry water from containers at the gate, filled each morning by a tanker. We have advanced from a two-holer toilet to a four-holer, from which the lizards crawling up the outside of the hessian walls look like iguanas.

The Fascist owner of the house in which the majority of us will live is about to arrive and take away his beautiful furniture, so things are pretty makeshift and topsy-turvy at the moment. Nan and I will work in God's office as before, a few yards along the footpath. The building is two-storeyed, with spacious living quarters downstairs for our warrant-officer and sergeant and two others. Next door is a generator which roars all day and half the night.

Across the road is the main Headquarters building where 'A' and 'Q' and Statistics and Central Registry and other branches are housed. Dotted around the blocks are others again — Dental and Medical and Pay and Post Office, the sergeants' mess, 'C' mess for the junior officers, 'B' mess for the more senior officers, and further afield in a grand and palatial old home is 'A' mess where our most senior officers, the majors and colonels and Brigadier Stevens, will abide in style.

In the town itself is the Garrison Theatre, and quite excitedly a group of us troop along to see George Formby in 'Bell-Bottom George', which is a terrible mistake. Do the entertainment people think the soldiers want or appreciate crudity? If so, they must be wrong because our Kiwi Concert Party is never crude and from what we hear it is the most popular of all concert parties. The South Africans are fine too, but the English are not all I thought them to be. Pukka blokes.

The Garrison Theatre has a ceiling consisting of two semi-circular slides which open up when the weather is suitable, so we will be able to see the moon put the stars to flight. Curfew is at 10 p.m., and after suffering George Formby we arrive at our mess at 10.30 so we have to waken the guard. Then, as all keys have been removed from the houses, we fiddle with a long wire to get inside our villa.

DAY TWO AND the colonel is just back from the Division with a great load of work. He takes time off to talk to me about the forthcoming summary of evidence and says he will see that Nancy travels with me to wherever it is held, as he doesn't like to think of my being alone. Neither do I. How I wish the date would come and go. Especially go.

After our talk I step out onto a balcony and there, alone and wrapped in misery, think how healing it would be to hear the magic mellifluous song of the tui, or even that raucous croak of his. But there is no birdsong in Italy, nor any birds. They have all been eaten. A sparrow would do, God. One cheeky little sparrow would do.

13

*I*T IS COLD when we set out at seven in the morning for Arezzo, 110 kilometres away. Very cold. The colonel from 'Q' is taking us there on his way to Siena. Nan and myself. For the summary of evidence.

The countryside is beautiful even in the rain, despite the twisted railway lines, the Bailey bridges, the forsaken remnants of Allied tanks and the shells of private homes. Briefly we stop at Perugia and buy postcards, 20 for the equivalent of one shilling, which tells us that the Americans have not reached town. At first sight I have fallen in love with Perugia with its university and other fine buildings, its winding streets and its steps.

Carrying on, we are caught up with several long stationary convoys and watch as Indians and Poles jump from the trucks to relieve themselves at the roadside. On behalf of Nan and myself, the colonel and our driver are embarrassed and apologetic.

On the outskirts of Arezzo we are delayed for half an hour by a Polish convoy which is understandably lost, as all signposts have been turned by the retreating Germans to face the wrong direction, some of them towards the sky. We ourselves become hopelessly lost trying to find the Town Major's office. All is chaos in the town.

When we do find the office, a soldier takes us to a building occupied by Italians, where there is a vacant room on the top floor. Nan and I can have that, the soldier says, raising his eyebrows, full of hope. But the colonel and Nan and I all shake our heads. No.

Eventually we find that we are booked in at the Officers' Transit Hotel, run by the British. In our Division we girls have the privileges of officers whether or not we are commissioned, so, though Nan is a private and I am a corporal, this is duly explained and accepted.

We are taken across the road and have a cup of tea with three Englishmen, who are hopelessly drunk. One winks at Nan and suggests she 'marry him, darling'. When she turns away muttering terrible things, he suggests that I do. Nan turns back and looks at him scathingly. And I laugh. I doubt that he is aware of either reaction.

Back in our room at the Transit Hotel we discover that the windows are broken and that there are sheets on Nan's bed and none on mine. The manager remedies this and says the Deputy Judge Advocate General, the DJAG, is downstairs waiting to have a few words with me about tomorrow's summary of evidence.

Major Robin Carl-Parker is indisputably a pukka sahib. He wears the most beautifully tailored uniform I have ever seen, with the shiniest buttons. Out of a cuff hangs a purple spotted handkerchief and neatly knotted at his neck is a matching cravat. He is very like a 'Two Type' cartoon character from the *Eighth Army News*: immaculate, overdressed, slightly ridiculous. Yet, despite his violently ginger hair, his monocle, and his seemingly effeminate and affected speech, Major Carl-Parker is most pleasant and sympathetic. Our few words stretch to two hours.

A tap on the bedroom door, and there stands the lethally handsome hotel manager.

'There's a small party on upstairs in the room of the Assistant Town Major. We'd like you both to come.' His eyes undress us.

Intrigued, we go. Anyone as handsome as this is conceited and therefore easy to handle, and Nan could handle him even if he were as plain as a wooden plank. The room we enter is large and in its centre is a colossal bed, one half draped with a mosquito net. On the other half a large dog lies, a setter of some sort. Half an hour later we escape, unscathed by man or dog.

Too late we discover that there is no water in the hotel. Containers of water are put in rooms each morning, but as we arrived in the afternoon we missed out. So we crawl into bed tired and unwashed. And cold. Even wearing a cardigan I am a block of ice, and this combined with the thought of the summary of evidence keep me awake all night.

We look forward to a good wash in the morning, but somehow we remain waterless. So I walk along the corridor, peep into a room whose door is open and see a bucket of water. Quickly I carry it to our room. As we go to breakfast I hear Major Carl-Parker tell the manager 'Some rascal's stolen my water. Can you see that some is put in my room, old man?'

We report to the summary of evidence room at 9.30 a.m. Major Carl-Parker is there, an Arab captain who is an interpreter, a court orderly, Akad the accused, an Arab escort, the kindly 'call me Cliff' lieutenant from the Palestinian unit, and Nan and myself. We are all sworn in and have a short break outside.

As the first witness I have a gruelling morning, and after lunch am questioned again, this time by the accused. There is a lot of shouting between the interpreter and the major and I am fearful they might even come to blows. Then Nan and Cliff give a short summary each and it is over.

Subdued, Nan and I walk around the poor dirty bombed town before returning to the hotel. I feel like the proverbial wrung-out dish-cloth, and while Nan offered no word of sympathy other than saying 'The bastard' as we left the courtroom, I know her so well that I am as conscious of her mental support as I am of her strong physical presence. And in fact I am pleased she is reticent about today's proceedings. It helps me not to wallow in self-pity and I am verging on the brink of that, ready to tip right over, which I mustn't do.

WE ARE GETTING ready for dinner when the colonel arrives unexpectedly and says, 'Be ready to leave in 10 minutes' time. I'm taking you to Florence.' We forget about dinner, pack our few bits and pay our bill of one and threepence each.

Through the pitch-black night we drive, but although Florence is only 130 kilometres away are held up by convoys and when finally we seem to be lost, the colonel asks for directions from an Italian driver. 'You are on the outskirts of Firenze, Sir.' We are there without knowing it.

A few more requests for directions and we are at the New Zealand Club, the Baglioni Hotel, where Nan and I are escorted to General Freyberg's room. The general not being in residence at the time, his room is ours! The lights are concealed, the bed is ornate, the walls are mirrored. There is a boudoir in which we can take the word literally and sulk if we wish. The bathroom is beautiful beyond description, and the curtains are made of linen and hand-made lace. A writing desk is at our disposal, and a glass-topped dressing table and divans. We decide that an ashtray is leaving with each of us. In memory.

'So this,' I say to Nan, 'is how the other half lives.'

Nan lies back on General Freyberg's bed and says, 'I like it. Especially for two shillings a night.'

We bathe. Oh, how we bathe. Dressing for dinner, I pull a long-tailed warm shirt over my head and am about to leave the room when I glance into a mirrored wall. The shirt-tail is so long I've forgotten to put on a skirt. At dinner the colonel tells us that tomorrow is ours and we return to Senigállia the following day.

At 9 a.m. we leave the hotel to look at the city but have gone only a few yards when the colonel appears beside us. He wants to buy gloves, he says, and my small hands will be useful. In the shop I try on glove after glove after glove while Nan, with her huge hands, wanders off behind fixtures and grimaces at me.

We yearn to buy leather and trinkets and shoes but have no money, so are pleased when the colonel lends us a thousand lire each.

As we look in a shop window, a young attractive Italian woman speaks to us in broken English. In her hand she holds a document she must present at the AMGOT (Allied Military Government of Occupied Territory) office to enable her to go to Rome. She has been several times, she explains, but each time had to stand in a long queue, leaving her baby in a pram outside, can we possibly help?

At the foot of the office steps two guards refuse to let the woman in the door, so Nan and I wave our arms and shout 'Presto' and they stand to attention and let us through. In two minutes the lady has her permit and spills tears over us.

We set out then for a symphony concert in which the orchestra has 32 violins, 16 basses and 12 brass and wood instruments. We hear Nicolai's 'Merry Wives of Windsor', Liszt's symphonic poem 'Les Preludes', Wagner's overture 'Die Meistersinger von Nürnburg' and Dvorak's 'Symphony No. 5 in E Minor'. Listening with closed eyes I am all but purring.

Returning to our club we pause at a shop window to admire a foot-high statue of 'The Boy with the Thorn in His Foot', priced beyond even the borrowed 1000 lire, but at exactly the right moment the colonel appears, listens to my drooling, and insists on lending me more money. Do you know what I do then? I cry because he is kind.

It seems to me that I have spent a lot of time crying lately, not always for reasons of happiness. Unhappiness and anger lurking close to the surface have also made me cry. It doesn't show too much, I hope. I try not to let it show.

I think about this. In our family we were trained to be independent, something I discover can be a handicap, because there are times I want very much to be anything but independent, want to lean on someone, to be consoled, to be loved in a special way. Others describe me as calm, not easily upset, but they don't know how little they know. Since Geoff was killed I have concentrated on concealing how I feel and smiling. How I smile! And I think a new thought till the moment passes. It becomes a habit and works pretty well. But not always.

After an early breakfast next day we are on the road for Senigállia, 'The Boy with the Thorn in His Foot' on my knee. Goodbye Florence.

'Sir,' says Nancy in one of her rare moments of respect, 'we could have made the other girls greener with envy if you'd let us stay another day to see the cathedral and art galleries.'

The colonel glares at her from the front seat. 'You were lucky to be here at all,' he says. 'Be grateful. Plenty of time to see it all, you'll see. It won't be long till we're stationed here.'

'Really!' Nan and I chorus. Stationed in Florence!

We are lost in the midst of a convoy of tank transporters. Two British provosts on motor cycles notice the Southern Cross emblem on our car. Mistaking us for a four-star general, they rev up their engines and, with sirens screaming, clear a lane for us through the traffic.

Soon we pass an Italian who has been run over, but the colonel will not stop. 'Only an Eyetie,' says he.

Then we see a pretty little girl of about seven. 'Just look at her,' I say. 'That hair, that nose, that mouth.'

'That tooth,' says the colonel from the front seat, his tone flat and teasing.

'You see,' Nan whispers to me, 'that's the quality you need to become a high-ranking officer. Bloody-mindedness.'

14
CHAPTER

*I*F YOU CLOSED your eyes and imagined Italy's beauty, you could think of her as virginally pure, wearing satin by day and velvet in the evening. How wrong you'd be. She is a whore, her legs widespread, and what she receives, asleep or awake, she does not receive with love. Every day and every night she is being raped, and she doesn't deserve that. She hasn't even been walking the streets. She has been at home minding her own business. Her father, the moon-faced Mussolini, loves her of course, but in watching her blossom under his paternal nurturing he does not perhaps realise that he is also witnessing her pain and his own demise. His orbed face grows rounder and rounder with power and/or vanity and/or a surfeit of pasta and *vino rosso*, and even as his daughter defends herself, he forgets that as fighters the Italians are very good violinists and opera singers.

The civilians we meet are remarkably serene. Those we know best work at our mess, Marcella, Rena and Gina. Marcella is older than the others, with an evil-looking *marito* who waits at the gate for her as she leaves for home, very often carrying vegetables she has stolen from the kitchen. Passing one of us, and holding our carrots or potatoes mid-air, she smiles disarmingly. 'Too much beautiful,' she says, sometimes pointing to our legs with her free hand, sometimes to our eyes.

Rena's husband has enlisted in the army and she has no idea whether or not he is alive. She has one of those resigned expressions which you know will remain the same if word comes that he has been killed. She is, you think, indestructible.

Little Gina is another matter, giggly and excitable, doing as she is told with a constant lovely smile, running, tripping, bumping into things, longing to be helpful. She is my special messenger in the dining-room. I have a weakness for roast potatoes, and I beckon her when I've finished my main course.

'Gina,' I say in my awful Italian, 'Per favore, vois parlare Signor Bob, possibile encora bruna potato per signorina Nivia?' Will she please ask Bob the cook for another roast potato for Neva? Giggling, she runs off and returns with not one roast potato, but two, still giggling, as if this little exercise is the most amusing thing in the world.

Along the muddy roadway from our mess is Peno the watchmaker, on whom we can totally depend. Any watch taken to him works perfectly for a day after its return and then stops dead. Peno and his mean, skinny black dog live in a narrow balconied house behind a high wooden fence. Peno is about 40, and wears a neat grey suit and dark glasses, be it day or night.

Benito is an 18-year-old who sits near us on the beach from time to time. Although a trifle overweight, he is a good-looking young man who sings beautifully and unselfconsciously as he doodles with a stick, pretending not to notice the four of us who swim almost every day.

Fabio is another 18-year-old who frequents the beach and sits nearby. In the briefest of bathing trunks the Italian men promenade, as they put it, but prefer not to get their feet wet. We have never seen Benito or Fabio enter the water.

It is surprising, then, to have Fabio approach our little group and say to me, 'You teach me to swim, I teach you Italian.'

This seems a good bargain, so into the water we go. I have Fabio lie face upward with my hands under his back and it is immediately clear that learning to float, let alone swim, is not what he has in mind. Nor is he interested in perfecting my atrocious Italian.

After the first so-called swimming lesson, one of our guards hands me an envelope with 'Miss Morrison' written shakily on it.

'You have an admirer,' he says. 'He's very shy.'

'I don't know anyone shy.'

'You do now,' says the guard.

The note is from Fabio. Here is what he writes:

Dear friend,
I don't know if you accept this letter bot is necessary who I say to you what my heart to bear love for you. I want to say to you whom I am in love, and you are my love.

I love you very much a long time. I wish to look you in sea, and every evening I promenade about your window for see the light in your room, the light whose you glare. To the night I cannot to sleep because I think of you.

Excuse me. It is possible you no to understand my letter because do not write

English very well. In this time I do mind being Italian because I can not stay whit you every time how an native of Zealand or English. I am very sad. I beg you no to think bad of me. I beg your pardon. I remember you every moment.
With love, Fabio
I trost and love you (I.T.A.L.Y.).

Fabio remains embarrassingly constant in his affection and it is difficult to see how he will ever graduate from the Naval College he is attending when he is on the beach so often.

We also know a small couple who live next door. Pietro is a tailor and his wife has a name very like Semolina, which is what I call her. Semolina is forever pregnant and in fear of miscarrying, but always wears a smile. As Pietro runs his tape measure up and down and around us in their bedroom, with his large machine on a table at the end of the bed, he is surrounded by fabrics and cottons and tissue paper, and scissors of all sizes, and tracing wheels, and pins and needles. Meanwhile, Semolina simply lies back against the pillows. This is the only way we ever see her so she might not have legs for all we know. As Pietro twitters and fusses, she lies, the lace bedspread draped high above her swollen middle.

Pietro glances at her from time to time and then at us. 'She is the most beautiful lady in Italy,' he says, and we nod in agreement. We are all liars. Semolina has a pale little pinched face, huge brown eyes, and her black hair hangs as straight as rain. She looks anaemic and undernourished, although she possibly eats an egg now and then if the two hens which seem permanent residents of the window-sill are anything to go by. Each time I am in Semolina's home I take her some chocolate, and I stroke the lovely lace bedspread and say, 'Will you leave this to me when you die?'

And Semolina smiles and answers, 'Si, si, signorina.'

We do make a brief attempt to learn to speak Italian properly. The professor is long and lean and lecherous, obviously thinking of more than *preposizioni e congiunzioni* or *verbi ausiliari*. He is thinking of all the bottoms he can pinch, which he does as he farewells us at the door after lessons one and two. There is no lesson number three. We decide we can get by without grammar.

NEVA, IN GISBORNE, 1939.

Neva after joining the army, Gisborne, 1942.

GEOFF PRIOR TO LEAVING NEW ZEALAND.

GISBORNE DRILL HALL STAFF. NEVA IS SIXTH FROM THE LEFT, SECOND ROW.

AT MIRAMAR CAMP, WELLINGTON, PRIOR TO SAILING. NEVA IS FOURTH FROM THE RIGHT, FRONT ROW.

The main waac mess
building, Santo
Spirito, 1944.

Neva outside the
Nissen hut, Santo
Spirito, 1944.

Above: OUTSIDE ST PETER'S, ROME. NEVA IS SEVENTH FROM LEFT.

Left: NEVA, SANTO SPIRITO, SOUTHERN ITALY.

MEMORIAL TO MAJOR THE
DOG, NEAR RIMINI.

A TRULLI HOUSE,
SOUTHERN ITALY.

Bridge of Sighs, Venice, 1945.

MAURINE AND NEVA HITCHHIKING.

TOPMOST TOWER OF SAN MARINO.

ITALIANS BY WRECKED HOMES, 1944. THE WOMEN HAVE RAGS TIED AROUND THEIR FEET.

Above: Theatre at
Senigallia, at which
they became
'extremely cultured'.

Right: Neva with
Senigallia maids, Gina,
Rena and the wicked
Marcella, 1944.

NANCY (STANDING) AND NEVA ON THEIR BALCONY, SENIGALLIA, 1944.

Jock Schofield, Neva's 'Cameron Highlander'.

Above: A TWO-MAN GERMAN SUBMARINE WASHED UP NEAR SENIGALLIA, 1944.

Left: NANCY AND NEVA IN THE DOORWAY OF HESSIAN EIGHT-HOLER TOILET AT SENIGALLIA, 1944.

Entertaining Sir Patrick Duff, UK High Commissioner in NZ, at the mess at Senigallia, 1945. Neva is third from right (standing). Sir Patrick is to her right. Brigadier (later General) Stevens is behind Neva.

Having a cup of tea on the move from Senigallia to Florence. Neva is second from left, back row.

BRIGADIER STEVENS AND LT-GENERAL SIR B. C. FREYBERG, VC, WALKING ALONG ONE OF THE MAIN ROADS NEAR THE NEW ZEALAND DIVISION HEADQUARTERS IN THE SENIO RIVER SECTOR, 1945. [*DA9110, War History Collection, Alexander Turnbull Library*]

15

CHAPTER

*A*LL OF US have grown fond of Senigállia, and of one another. We have had time, now, to appreciate our similarities and our differences, and generally speaking we are nonjudgemental. June and Joyce and Betty are the closest, as they had been in camp together in Auckland for quite a while. We others were thrown together at WAAC Camp in Wellington. There, Maurine and Dorraine from Invercargill were allotted to one hut, shared a room in Santo Spirito, and now share another in Senigállia. Nan and I were bracketed because we travelled from the East Coast, Nan from Napier, I from Gisborne. But even those who were not paired off fit in perfectly and some are very special, like Minerva with her beauty, and Lucy with hers, breaking hearts with her curls, her sparkling blue eyes and black lashes, and her natural sweetness. Marge and Edna are like twins, although they had not met previously. Thel and our OC, Dot, came from Army Headquarters in Wellington. Mayse, one of the three who are much older than the rest of us, is tall and willowy and very often amusing. Auckland's Peg drifts amongst us all but seems happiest with those of us who swim. She is great company and often joins Thel and Nan and me in a poetry-reading session, into which we retreat to escape from a round of parties.

I conceal much that I feel most of the time, because doing so makes living at close quarters with others peaceful rather than confrontational. But Nan and I voice petty annoyances to each other. Rock of Gibraltar that she is, she would never divulge. She is far too loyal for that. Like a fighting cock, she would stand up to anyone who criticised a friendship she valued, which includes my own. Yet, I ask myself, do I really know even Nan?

It is a strange closeness we all have, an unnatural one. Friends at home were like old clothes, something you were comfortable with and understood to the extent that you knew the warp and weft of their thinking. Here emotions are dressed in a stranger's clothes and although you live with the wearer and are aware of her speech patterns, her eating habits, the way she walks, still you do not quite know her. Uniforms are all the same (other than Min's), jackets reach so many inches below the waist, buttons are spaced exactly the same distance apart, epaulettes sit like this, berets like that, shoes are indistinguishable (although I swear mine outshine the rest) and no one's hair (other than Min's) touches the collar, but these things are only what are offered to the onlooker, what is visible. As we live together, enriched for the most part, our other selves are hidden behind the similarities we are content not to disturb.

I doubt that I truly know myself, and won't until the curtain comes down on the stage and reality is faced. In critical moments I also doubt that some girls realise how unreal our being here is, a strutting on the stage as we fill the role required of us. I wonder if they consider how much each of us must have changed since leaving New Zealand.

Sometimes I am shocked at my own thinking. I would prefer to be surprised because to me shock is negative and surprise positive. If a man kills his wife I am shocked and would like to know that he will hang until he is very dead. Surprises are boxes of chocolates from someone you didn't know cared, three dandelions picked for you by a child, a breathlessly beautiful sunset over a low horizon or, if you are especially lucky, falling in love across a crowded room.

And so, while we know one another so well, in a way we don't at all. Soldiers in a slit trench are another matter, but we are not soldiers in slit trenches. We are doing secretarial work as we did at home, but in a very different environment. It is our reaction to being here that is responsible for the unknown qualities in our personalities, and in a way this not knowing is comfortable while it is confusing. There is no fear of being disappointed in someone if you don't know all there is to know about her. The hidden areas are a kind of insurance policy against that.

Taking dictation from the military secretary, I voice this thought. Much more worldly than I, he looks at me, mystified. 'What is there to be confused about?' he asks. 'You're all here doing a damned fine job exactly as you were in New Zealand. You're the same people, girl.'

'But we've been transplanted.'

'So?'

'We're in another world. We're not little cabbages in a home garden any more. We're something else, and what that is I don't know. Of course it's confusing.'

'It shouldn't be,' the colonel answers with utter certainty.

'Maybe you're in too lofty a position to understand.' Belatedly I add, 'Sir'.

'Do you think of me as lofty?'

'We all do. We're in awe of you.' I smile widely as I speak. This was true, at least of me, when I first arrived in Italy. The sight of this black-bereted man walking briskly into the office carrying a fat bundle of files under an arm and totally ignoring us had intimidated me then. Now I see past his confidence and his rank and discover a perfectly approachable human being.

He shakes his head at me. 'You girls in awe of anybody! No need to lie to me, Neva Yvonne.'

16

*I*N SEPTEMBER THE troops were fighting fiercely north of Rimini, where mines were embedded in ditches and stopbanks and canals, and booby traps and mud and rain hindered our men. The Rubicon of old was flooded, so it was necessary to reroute until finally reaching Cesena. The line was held by anti-tank gunners, as there was a shortage of infantry and cavalry. Late in October they were withdrawn.

There is no real rest of course. In late November and in icy winds and frequent snowstorms, the reinforced troops passed through Forli to take up positions facing Faenza, which was cleared by the Ghurkas. By mid-December our men had reached the Senio River.

This campaign has cost more than 400 lives and almost two thousand wounded. Because we are slowly pushing the Germans back, all this slaughter is called winning the war, I suppose. It doesn't bear thinking of.

One good piece of news is that our prisoners of war at Bologna are being transferred to an Oflag in Germany. I am particularly interested because my sister's fiance is one of these men. To be truthful I am pleased he is a prisoner. Surely there is more chance of an infantry officer surviving as a prisoner of war than there would be otherwise.

We knew Bill had taken over Errol Williams' dog, Major, their regimental mascot, when Errol was killed, and I have often wondered what happened to Major when Bill was captured. Now I know.

On one of our hitchhiking days, Maurine and I jumped from the back of a truck near Rimini, and there on the roadside was the grave of Major, or as the inscription on the black diamond read: 'No. 1 Dog, Major MAJOR. Regimental Mascot 19th NZ Armd Regt 3rd Oct 1939–17th Dec 1944. Campaigns Libya 1941, Egypt 1942, Italy 1943. Died of Sickness 17th Dec 1944.'

I had with me my Purma camera, a gift from Geoff on my nineteenth birthday — 'a Purma-nent record of my love,' his note had said. I photographed the inscription and was filled with emotion as I thought of Bill, of my sister, and of Geoff. Memories of other days crowded my mind, a mixture of joy and sadness.

For Maurine and me, our one hitchhiking day a week is a highlight. We have an early breakfast and are out on the road with a satchel on our shoulder containing our lunch — usually a tin of bully beef, an apple and some coffee. At times we plan a destination, but often simply aim at going as far as we can while being able to get back to the mess before the gates close.

Maurine smokes but I don't, so I take all the cigarettes that have been allotted to me to use in bartering. At home a private's daily rate of pay was five shillings but overseas it has risen to six shillings a day, still not enough to fill even a small sock with purchases. As we are often paid the equivalent of one shilling for a single cigarette, I am delighted that I am a non-smoker. Were I not, I would quickly become one. Another thing I use for bartering purposes is my dark Patriotic chocolate issue which I detest. Thankfully the Italians don't mind whether chocolate is light or dark. As long as it is chocolate, that is fine with them.

One day we go first to the post office and clamber into the mail truck going to the Division. After an hour of sitting on mail bags, we are dropped off and then picked up by South Africans going to Rimini. There a redcap puts us on two English trucks in a large convoy, each of us sitting in front with the driver, so for a change we can see where we are going instead of where we've been. The edges of the road are marked 'Mines', and just after passing two burnt-out aircraft the convoy stops for some time near a main corner. Maurine and I are about to ask the help of a redcap when a South African in a jeep nods at us.

'Are you going to San Marino?' we ask.

'No.'

'Oh,' we say, disappointed, 'we are.'

The South African speaks to the jeep's other occupant and says, 'We'll take you half way.'

We are quick to climb into the vehicle lest they have second thoughts. As soon as they put us down, an English staff car driver takes us through the Siera Valley. We pass a field in which a ploughman and his ox have just been blown up, all that remains of the beast being the horns. The man is a gory spread-eagled mess, only just recognisable as a human being. His head is missing altogether. Along with nausea, a wave of anger passes through me. That field had to be ploughed and the farmer ploughed it but he was no part of any war, which makes his death sadder, less forgivable.

To reach the town of San Marino itself we climb hundreds of steps to the top of the steep cliffside where a redcap asks us for our passes, the tiny independent Republic of San Marino being neutral and out of bounds.

'We're not allowed to be in Rimini yet,' we explain, 'let alone having a pass to enter San Marino.'

'Go right ahead,' the redcap says. 'You deserve to get in.' We hurry by.

Very hungry, we are taken to an inn by some South Africans and sit overlooking the valley below, the Rubicon snaking its way into the distance. With the permission of the proprietor, we produce from our satchels a bumper lunch — coffee, a tin of meat and vegetables (or M and V as we called it), beans, spam and fruit and cream. The proprietor smiles with astonishment at the quantity and assortment of food we consume.

Before leaving the inn we each have a sticky Strega liqueur to repay him for his kindness, and then climb the town's peak, from which, on this wonderfully clear day, we can see Yugoslavia. Each rooftop in the Republic has the Geneva Convention white cross on it. The Germans respect this, and their navigators are more accurate than those of the Americans, who dropped a bomb on the building next to the Regent's Palace and made a nasty mess of it.

In all of Italy this is the only place in which shopkeepers prefer money to soap, cigarettes or chocolate. The residents have all they need, beautiful clothes and food, their income being derived largely from the sale of postage stamps.

Inside the palace we sit in the Regent's chair and sign the visitor's book — Maurine from Invercargill, the most southern town in New Zealand, and I from Gisborne, the most eastern. Still being kind to us, the South Africans take us down the hill in their jeep. I am left feeling as I did after seeing the trulli country in southern Italy, as if I am part of a fairy tale. That is, until we pass the site of the mine accident. Now the area is taped off and sappers are sweeping within the boundary. A sack has been thrown over the farmer's body.

The South Africans have not finished with their kindness, inviting us to their mess where we have dinner before they drive us back to Senigállia. Our OC does not believe us when we offer our excuse for being late in getting back — that we were held up for an hour because a tank transporter had become stuck on a Bailey bridge and there was no way we could get past it.

Another town we aim at seeing is Riccione. A huge negro in a tiny jeep offers us a ride, which we turn down, and we wait and wait. When two Kiwi dispatch riders come along on motor cycles, in desperation we decide to do the forbidden and become pillion riders.

Riccione is sad. Buildings lean at such strange angles you can imagine a footfall will see them tumble. As rows of huge and ugly Churchill tanks rumble through the streets on their iron tracks, the noise is deafening.

Canadians in a jeep bring us back as far as Catolica and invite us to tea at their mess, which sits in a sea of mud. There they have a mascot, a five-year-old Italian boy they found in a trench at Cassino wearing nothing but a smile. He had lived with Germans and spoke little Italian, and now, clad in a Canadian battledress and speaking English, he tells us, 'Don't speak to me Eyetie. I'm a Canadian.' As we leave he advises us to, 'Take it easy.'

Back at our mess a lot of mail from home awaits us, including baking. We all pool our offerings and eat everything in sight and feel very satisfied.

The rosy glow dies rapidly at the office in the morning. In a casualty list I type is the name of a Gisbornite — 'Both legs amputated below the knee.' He is luckier than the Italian ploughman, of course. He is alive and will return home on a hospital ship.

Two Gisbornites dined at our mess three nights ago. Now one of them calls. He is alone.

'Our tank was hit,' he says. 'I jumped one way. Brian jumped the other way. That's how it is. If you turn the wrong way to piss you could cop it. I didn't get a scratch but . . .' He hesitates. 'Brian's head was blown off.' He turns away.

I am stunned as I think of Brian, a Duntroon graduate. And I think of his mother and father who used to give me a ride to work when it was raining. Nice people. Kind people. Writing to them I will say softening things, some of which might not be true. Certainly I will tell them of Brian's meal at our mess, because from experience I know such things are helpful, even cherished. They are more easily understood than a message from a commander saying a son's life was laid down with selflessness, or a cable from the King expressing gratitude for a life so nobly given. Nobly given? What did the King know? Or any commander? Brian didn't want to lay down his life with selflessness or give his life nobly or otherwise. He wanted to go home, but he wouldn't be doing that. Because *c'est la guerre. C'est la* bloody *guerre.*

17

CHAPTER

*S*ID THE PROVOST is with us this time. We are on our way to Arezzo for the court-martial and I wish someone knew how I feel. I am in the back seat of the staff car. It would be comforting to have my father's shoulder close to mine but it isn't there. Just the same it would be worse if Nancy wasn't sitting alongside me, and I am grateful to the military secretary who decided that her coming was wise. My throat is taut.

As we drive I am quiet, remembering to smile slightly. Geoff's vain Auntie Sadie once told me that her serene expression came from imagining someone was always looking at her. I am trying to practise that now, because I know that if I don't my face will crumple and tears will ooze from where they lurk behind my eyelids. Sometimes I am aware that Nancy is glancing at me. Beside the driver sits Sid the Provost, saying nothing. He is in a foul mood for some reason, perhaps for no reason.

At six in the evening we arrive at the office of the Arezzo Town Major. Nancy and I sit in chairs provided, but Sid leans against a desk looking as if he loathes everything and everyone. He does not listen to instructions about the court-martial, just stares at the wall as if he is above that sort of thing. Being told what to do? Poof!

'Perhaps he's constipated,' Nancy says later. Neither of us cares a lot.

The court-martial begins at 9.30 in the morning and moody Sid travels there in the staff car, leaving Nan and me to paddle through the rain on foot. As a diversionary tactic I try to concentrate on this, on Sid's pettiness in the midst of a war in which thousands of his countrymen are being killed.

In the courtroom Major Carl-Parker and his interpreter sit at one side of a long table, with the defence lawyer and his interpreter opposite. At the head of the table three court members flank the judge advocate. The accused is there looking nervous, his escort is there looking nervous, Mac is there looking extremely nervous, and I am there, very, very nervous. A court orderly stands

74

waiting, for what I wonder? Instructions? Handing pieces of paper from this person to that? We shall see. The atmosphere is tense.

After being questioned from 9.30 till noon by Major Carl-Parker, I feel distressed and very pale. As we leave the courtroom to adjourn for lunch I notice that Nancy and Sid, who have been sitting in a hallway, are saying nothing to each other. I soften towards Sid, wondering if he is nervous rather than arrogant, but quickly dismiss this thought, suspecting that he is anxious to be called to give evidence so he can feel important and is mentally rehearsing what he will say and how he will say it. As I smile weakly at Nan the orderly hands me a note from 'call me Cliff' of the Palestinian Arab unit. He intended to be here, he writes, but is in hospital with jaundice. He hopes things go well for me.

After lunch Mac is questioned, and is so like a terrified kitten and looks so alone and forlorn I wish someone would say something comforting to him, but this is no place for pleasantness.

Nancy and Sid the Provost are questioned briefly and Sid tells me he was congratulated on his report. It is to be hoped this will sweeten him up slightly.

It is my turn then to be cross-examined by Akad's defence lawyer. For some reason this involves much shouting and arguing between him and Major Carl-Parker and between them both and the judge advocate.

When I am asked to repeat what Akad said to Mac on the roadside before I was carried off by the other two soldiers, I hesitate.

'I'm sorry,' I explain, my voice small. 'One word I can't repeat.'

'Print it on this piece of paper,' says the judge. The orderly hands me a sheet of foolscap.

'In capital letters,' orders the judge.

In capital letters, I print the word F U C K.

The paper is handed back to the judge who looks up and around us all. 'Fuck,' he announces in a loud voice. A clearly audible titter passes round the room and I feel humiliated and stupid and dirty.

I am also very angry. Bloody men! How dare they titter? They don't know what it's like.

It gets worse. Why were you and this young man in such a remote area? There was no reason to go to an isolated spot for anything other than sex, was there? Aren't you girls here to provide sex for your own men? How old are you? Nobody is going to believe you are a virgin. Are you a virgin, Miss Morrison?

On and on it goes, until at almost four o'clock Akad is questioned and the shouting in Arabic becomes louder and louder. Arms are waved and fingers are pointed at me and speakers glance in my direction from time to time and I don't know what is going on in this foreign tongue.

Then I hear the judge advocate say four beautiful unmistakeable words. 'Five years hard labour,' he announces sternly. Suddenly it is over and I swallow hard with relief. Voices quieten. Papers are shuffled, chairs are pushed back and as everyone stands up in preparation to leaving the courtroom Akad steps forward, pausing to stare at me with calculated hatred in his eyes.

Outside I feel washed white and wrung out and worthless, and when Nan squeezes my arm my smile is weak. Her touch, her kindness, bring tears to my eyes.

A few days after the court-martial a note is delivered to our headquarters from the Palestinian Arab headquarters suggesting that I be alerted to a possible reprisal by Akad's two associates. However, the troops are rapidly advancing, the Palestinian Arab unit has gone north to somewhere unknown and we have moved from Santo Spirito to Senigállia, and no such thing has eventuated to date.

It doesn't surprise me to receive a letter from Mac soon after the court-martial, again apologising. I can blame the rapid advancing of the troops for my losing track of him. I regret this, but one thing I know. He will always remember the unfortunate episode as I do, although in an entirely different way, and perhaps not as often. And remembering, he will still feel apologetic, I am certain, because he is that sort of person. A gentleman.

18
CHAPTER

SOME INTERESTING THINGS are happening. I type reports about Cassino and am surprised that General Freyberg writes as if the Germans are brainless, which we know they are not. And if they are, why did we get so badly beaten there?

Another thing is that the experiment in sending our Clerical Division girls overseas has apparently been judged a success by whoever reviews such things, probably Brigadier Stevens and Army Headquarters in Wellington. Another hundred secretaries are to join us, many to work at Maadi and some in Italy. Dot will go back to Egypt and one of us will be commissioned and take over from her here. We talk about this amongst ourselves and decide the honoured girl will be chosen from the three oldest in our group. Certainly one is smiling more than usual and wears a slight look of authority, as if quite confident of being named.

Who takes over doesn't trouble me because our lives will go on much as before. What concerns me more is that the 'i' on my typewriter has fallen off and I am waiting for the 'i' specialist to arrive and fix it. By now any New Zealand farmer would have had the matter remedied with a piece of No. 8 fencing wire.

June is going home because her young sister is terminally ill. We'll all miss her so much, not only because she is such a fine secretary, but because she never complains and is philosophical when minor things go wrong, and she has a sense of the ridiculous and is fun to be near. And candidly not everyone is quite as lovable as that. Her two Auckland roommates will feel a gap in their lives, as will one or two males.

There have been some dreadful films showing at the Garrison Theatre, but we go just the same. Last night as several of us watched Abbott and Costello in *Keep 'em Flying*, it began to rain heavily. The roof, which had been open to the sky, refused to close, so we were all drenched, which made things worse than they already were.

We have had a visit from the Kiwi Concert Party who are very, very good, unlike the films at the theatre. We have promised to give them some of our new white mosquito nets to dye and make into frocks for their female impersonators. After their show we go to supper at 'B' mess and eat hot toast, chicken and hard-boiled eggs.

I have had an influx of Gisborne visitors. One sings and dances divinely, I went to primary school with another, the third was a schoolteacher and the fourth a bank clerk. And on the inside of a cigarette packet delivered to me is a message from a friend in the Young Farmers Club, Rowley Smith. He is in our First General Hospital down the road and asks that I visit him, which I do. He is severely wounded everywhere but in his head and left arm. As his right arm is badly fractured and he can't hold a pen, he would like me to write home for him. His brother was killed in the Air Force in 1940, and he is very concerned for his mother and wants her to be reassured. So I shall do my best, tell her that my writing is only temporary, that her son is very cheerful, which he is, and that I'll write again soon.

All around us men in beds are — what is the word? — chiacking. Laughing and joking anyway. Leaving the ward, I turn back and wave, thinking how extraordinary it is that in a military hospital, where rows of men lie slightly or shockingly wounded, there is more light-heartedness than I have seen anywhere, ever before.

We have formed a little choir, which is not at all bad. The accoustics are dreadful at the hospital theatre where we practise carols night after night. Wearing our best uniforms, we walk at last through the wards, we girls holding the score sheets as our male counterparts follow us carrying candles so we can see what we are reading. We sing 'While Shepherds Watched Their Flocks by Night', 'Christians Awake', 'Hark! The Herald Angels Sing', 'O Come All Ye Faithful', 'Once in Royal David's City', 'Good King Wenceslas', 'The First Nowell', and finally 'Silent Night'.

At the end of our performance a nursing sister approaches me. 'Your cousin wants to speak to you,' she says, and leads me down the ward where all I can see of the face of a man are two holes for eyes, two for nostrils and one for a mouth. All else is swathed in bandages.

'Hello, cousin,' the man says.

' You look a bit of a mess.'

The soldier waits until the sister walks away.

'I had to say you were my cousin,' he says then, 'or she mightn't have given you my message. I wanted to say your singing was lovely.'

'I just like to sing.'

'Will you come and visit me soon?' the soldier asks. 'I'd like that.' The voice is faint. The card at the end of the bed tells me it belongs to William Edgar Harris, aged 24, of whom I have never heard.

'Of course,' I say. In a couple of days' time.'

We girls do not discover until we are back at the mess that we have thick blobs of candle grease down the backs of our dress uniforms.

19

*O*UR CATHOLIC GIRLS attend a civilian church. We others join our men at a service held in a hall in the village. The piano is played by anyone capable of doing so, and one of our girls does this at times.

We wear our dress uniforms to church even when we also have to wear gumboots, and that is often right now. The onslaught of winter is upon us and mud, mud is everywhere.

Back at the mess after one service we find Canadian Gumboot Charlie, patiently waiting to give us a box of apples. Last time it was oranges. He is in Supplies and gave Maurine and me a lift on one of our hitchhiking trips, when he was transporting English gumboots.

The food he brings us is most appreciated, not only by the girls, but by Bob the cook. Bob steals our Andrews Liver Salts from Red Cross parcels to use as baking powder and welcomes any additional food brought to us by friends. A wild looking fellow from the West Coast, it is he who boils the water for our baths outside in a drum. And it is he who secretly brings Nan and me a cup of tea each morning in our bedroom next to the kitchen. The noise from his burner wakes us early, which makes us decide to go for a brisk walk before breakfast every day, wearing our raincoats over our pyjamas. The minute Bob hears us return, in he comes with the tea and a leery look. He has almost always been very drunk the night before.

We have no complaints about Bob's meals, partly because we are always so hungry, and when a special occasion arises he excels. At Christmas time we are going to be surprised, he tells us. All he will divulge is that we will have Christmas pudding and brandy sauce. Is there a war on, we wonder?

The day arrives. Christmas Day, 1944. Most of us are in the lounge when there is a knock on the door. There stands a small Italian woman accompanied by a fierce looking young male who demands to see Bob. Anxious to see what the fuss is about, we girls gather in the hallway.

'They've lost a bloody turkey,' Bob says. 'Let's look for it.'

Out of the house we all go, searching up and down the street and through the grounds of both our properties, even in our hessian *gabinetto*. There is not a turkey in sight, so, grumbling and glowering, the Italians depart.

In the dining room the table is beautifully set, with a small posy in the centre, provided by Marcella says she with a proud smile. 'Too much beautiful, signorini.' The oyster soup is faultless, as are the 'angels on horseback'. Then comes the main course: roast and mashed potatoes, cauliflower with sauce, green peas, roast pork, roast duck and roast . . .

'Bob,' cries Dot our OC, 'What is this?'

Bob hurries from the kitchen. 'That, ma'am, is roast turkey,' he beams.

As we eat it we spare a thought for the Italians, but forget them as we progress to the Christmas pudding with brandy sauce followed by beer and nuts and oranges and coffee. Bob really does us proud when he tries.

THERE IS THE usual round of end-of-year parties. One is at an English unit at Fano where a notice warns that German parachutists are expected and also seaborne saboteurs. The unit is on the alert, which is nice to know as it is responsible for the protection of Senigállia.

Another party is at 'A' mess, whose members are so senior they are expected to be faultless, and it is amusing to watch their behaviour. Some unbend with dignity but others fail dismally. Brigadier Stevens surprises us all by sitting on a table with the military secretary and singing Christmas carols, and, apparently tiring of lovely Lucy calling him 'Sir', suggests she doesn't.

'What shall I call you then, Sir?' she asks, expecting him to say, 'Bill'.

'Call me Brig,' he says and goes on singing carols.

20
CHAPTER

JOCK WITH THE kilt is being most attentive. When he comes south he brings us food so is very popular. He is dominating my life, dropping in unexpectedly, taking me to dances and films and operas in the evening and telephoning almost every day. He was at our mess one evening when another English officer was there, and neither spoke to the other.

'Why?' I asked Jock.

'He's artillery, Neva. I'm infantry.'

'What does it matter? We have every kind of person at our mess.'

'Ah, but we English don't,' Jock said.

'Isn't that slightly crazy?' I asked, and all Jock did was shrug.

Time passes and Jock makes a special visit to tell me he has broken his engagement to a girl back home, a friend of the family. Their betrothal had been announced when they were 21, but now he knows he can never marry anyone but me.

How to react to this? I've been a friend, a good one I hope. But I have a lot of friends, some of whom are exactly like him, imagining you are in love with them because they are in love with you. How often have I explained that this is a foreign environment, not a place to decide on futures, and suggested we just leave things as they are? As the months pass this conversation with Jock takes place over and over again, and then he folds me in his arms so I reach exactly to the top of his uniform pocket, and he kisses me with such gentleness and love it should be overwhelming. And then I think of Geoff. Why can't I stop wearing him like a second skin? Why can no other man make me feel even vaguely as he did? Why can't Jock, in whose eyes I can do no wrong, set a spark alight? He is everything I like, has an appealing personality, and is fond of his parents and his sister and brother. He is honest and kind and loyal; he is tall and fair and handsome; and he is here. Is there something wrong with me? I have no way of knowing the answer, if indeed there is one. Emotions are so puzzling, so elusive.

Sometimes I look at other girls I know well yet don't know, and wonder about their emotions. Like Nancy. She retains her apparent loathing of officers, being surrounded always by privates or corporals and an occasional sergeant. Yet she does have one friend who is an English captain. What he has that other officers haven't she never reveals. No questions are asked and no explanations given. Nancy never interferes with another's life or even thinking, and expects others to behave that way towards her, and we do. Even after rooming with her for so long there are parts of Nancy that are complete blanks to me.

I can not help wonder at times how some girls behave with their men friends. You could say we have opportunities galore to be promiscuous, yet at the same time, none at all. We are thrown together closely, and the attractions are undeniably there, but the geography is missing. If sex is what you want the site to indulge in it is not readily available. Certainly our bedrooms are out of bounds, as one young officer discovers to his detriment after wandering along an upstairs hallway in an inebriated state and being gleefully reported by our guards. Who he was looking for perhaps even he did not know.

'He's weak, of course,' someone says.

'You'd expect more of an officer,' says someone else.

With no expression whatever Nan says. 'I could name plenty of weak officers.'

As angels in God's office, she and I have typed many an adverse report on weak officers, officers contracting VD and so on. The unrelenting Nan has evidence to support her opinion.

If other girls are tempted sexually, so am I. It isn't easy to resist Jock and some others when the pull is strong and the flesh weak. But I recall something which is very important to me. My sister and I were in the changing sheds at Waikanae Beach and eavesdropping on a conversation taking place through the wall in the male section. Two young men were talking about girls they'd taken out and we listened with fascination.

Then, 'Neva Morrison,' one voice said. 'You never get any change out of her.'

My sister and I stifled our laughter in our towels.

I want it to stay that way in Italy, don't want men I am not especially fond of getting any change out of me, don't want to be talked about by what I call the 'kiss and tell' brigade, and there are plenty of those around, I am certain.

I suspect some girls feel differently and ask myself, if beds are out, where? The back seat of a car? You'd need a senior officer for that and, well, we have senior officers. Food for thought. And then there are the beauties like Min and Lucy.

You can't possibly be as attractive as they are and not have men keen to bed you down. It is out of the question.

When Min goes to hospital to have her appendix out I wonder anew. Appendicitis? But after three days in hospital she arrives at the mess for a few hours, and soon afterwards a friend of hers from the Division arrives in a tank. Min has always wanted a ride in a tank, so the two walk out to the road and Min has a foot raised to get into the machine when a head appears from a window in the Medical Section next door where she works, and her senior officer shouts, 'Min, you've just had your appendix out. Take your foot off that tank, girl, or you'll split your stitches.'

Jock is on another visit south and as we chat by the top of the office stairs the military secretary interrupts us, handing me a piece of paper.

I glance at it as he turns to leave and my hand goes to my mouth. 'Come back,' I cry.

The colonel comes back, as if I am the master and he the servant.

'This can't be true.'

'Of course it's true. You're a pretty damned efficient person, the right one for the job, and you've got it. The choice was unanimous.' He looks at Jock and says, 'She's just been commissioned. No doubt you approve.'

'Absolutely.' Jock's grin is very wide.

Later Jock says, 'You see, you're very special. I'm so proud of you, Neva. Please. Please say you'll marry me.'

'I can't. I just can't.'

'You will,' he says. He is as sure as that.

DORRAINE SAYS, 'LET'S go along to the hospital to see Joye.'

Joye, one of the latecomers who has joined us, has trench mouth and is extremely miserable, but looks palely pretty sitting against her pillows.

I leave her for a time to visit the man who called me his cousin when we were singing Christmas carols — Sergeant William Edgar Harris, aged 24. After walking up and down the ward without seeing him I conclude that he has been moved to another ward or sent home, so check with the nursing sister.

She shakes her head and puckers her nose. 'Your cousin died on Boxing Day,' she says. 'I'm so sorry.'

I feel bad about this. If Jock was killed I'd feel even worse, and he is about to go off to the second front. Any day now he'll be gone. Can I let him go without returning his affection? How would I feel if he leaves without hope and dies as this fictitious cousin of mine has? My emotions are in further turmoil.

Before long Jock comes to say a very earnest goodbye. He says he will always love me in a way he had never imagined he could, and if I don't like the thought of living in England he will be quite happy to come to New Zealand to work.

Is it this that sways me? Do I subconsciously want to live always in my home country? I don't think so. What I do think is that this kilted man, who has shown me nothing but kindness, is big enough in his heart to leave his own homeland, position and family to please me. What I could expect from him would always be that generosity of spirit and the warmth of his love. He is not demanding as some others are, but giving. All along the line giving. And I am selfish and unappreciative and unkind towards one of the loveliest human beings I have ever met.

'You will say yes, Neva, won't you?'

'Yes. I will say yes.' A small voice inside me asks, Do you understand, Geoff? I'm not entirely sure that I do.

Jock's state of elation disturbs me. There is so much he doesn't understand and I can not possibly tell him about the torch I still carry for Geoff. I can see that he imagines I feel exactly as he does, which I wish were true, but it isn't. That is something else I can not possibly tell him.

21

*N*OW I AM in charge, I am no longer in God's office but across the road in the main administration building. My room is off an upstairs balcony, with windows looking down over other offices and a number of Italian homes. The brigadier and his staff are to my right and Central Registry to my left. Downstairs are 'A' and 'Q' branches.

Apart from a typewriter, on my desk a pile of paybooks waits for me to organise inoculations for all the girls, papers of all kinds fill pigeon-holes, and pencils wearing pink rubber hats sit alongside a bottle of Stephens very black ink. My favourite fountain pen is there too, with a wide-spreading nib which puts character into handwriting. The pen was a 21st birthday present from my sister. It is muted greys, blues and pinks, and it lives in a snakeskin wallet which has a small pocket in it for stamps, a larger one for coins and a third for banknotes, should you happen to have any.

Most importantly, a series of registers sits there, and a pile of pink and blue and white signals and ciphers I must deal with and then have distributed by Central Registry or by myself, depending on their urgency and importance. The room is full of maps which are in total disorder. Men come in from other offices and from the Division and take forever to find the maps they want. So I will somehow sort them out in a way that at least I can understand, which should simplify things for everyone and also make the air less profane than it is now.

God, Colonel McGlashan, sees fit to bring me work from across the road, perhaps feeling that as my fate as an officer now lies in his hands he can order me about. Our lovely Presbyterian padre visits me with the news that the colonel, who attends a church service on the third Sunday each January, one of which is about to come up, has requested that I sing a solo. Protesting vigorously, I claim that I have a tickling throat, that I am nervous in the extreme, that noises on the road outside the hall represent too much opposition and that I am unhappy singing solos.

Colonel McGlashan strides across the road. 'What's this nonsense about not singing in church? Of course you'll sing.' I sing in church.

The Fifth Reinforcements are on their way home and four Gisbornites call in to say goodbye, including a cousin, Ted. A real cousin. They are very happy and very drunk.

We all go to see the Rome Opera Company's *La Traviata*, a rendition much sadder than intended. The hero, who has been neglectful of the heroine for a long time, re-enters her life conscience-stricken, emerging from the wings to find her singing weakly on the opposite side of the stage as she dies slowly of consumption. Overcome with contrition and belated affection he rushes across the stage, and as he clasps her to his bosom they crash to the floor in an untidy heap, legs and arms askew. Singing on, their voices remain exquisite.

A quiet girl and her fiance knock on my door and ask if they can have a word or two. I say of course, what do they want, to borrow my primus, some coffee and milk or something else? It is none of these things. The girl wants to be married to this soldier right away, and in a mosquito net. I express more joy than I feel as I listen to the girl explain that we can gather together a few of our new fine white nets which have replaced the heavy thick green we had previously and have the man next door with the wife and the hens make a wedding frock.

Nan and I are appalled as we discuss being married overseas, letting any brand-new husband see our awful army underwear and massive striped pyjamas, and especially the bras that look like floorcloths and flatten any bosom you might have. The father of the prospective bride is mayor of somewhere in the deep south of New Zealand, and we are sure her mother would visualise something more glamorous than a faded pink cotton floorcloth holding up her daughter's magnificent honeymoon bosom.

'I don't suppose she thought she'd see the day she got married in a mosquito net either,' I say.

Nan says, 'I think she might prefer the frock to the husband. She's much nicer than he is. Much more "rayfeened".' It is true and we are sad.

Fortunately, the daughter is happy not to do a thing until she tells her parents her good news, and we are all relieved when a letter comes which persuades the couple to wait until they return home before finalising anything.

'Obviously her mum and dad want to see what their daughter's getting herself into,' Nan reasons. And I agree. And approve. Besides which, our mosquito nets are safe.

22
CHAPTER

*I*N A WAY I don't enjoy working alone in my room as much as I did in the military secretary's office, where there was company with whom to share laughter and conversation at odd moments. It is conversation our men from the Division yearn for, conversation of a familiar kind, about people and places back home, but also about feelings they prefer not to mention to males lest they be judged wanting in some way. A sergeant who comes to my office often is a wreck as he confides in me yet again.

'Tell me about being afraid?' I ask, because I have learned an important truth, that if a soldier feels you sincerely understand something of his inner turmoil, he is relieved to answer intimate questions.

The sergeant hesitates, looking at me, wondering, summing me up. 'I've been bloody scared every minute I've been in battle,' he says then. 'Especially at fucking Cassino. You were pretty sure you were a goner there.' His voice is soft. Suddenly he hangs his head and begins to sob. He does not seem to notice that I have taken his hand.

'You won't tell, will you? The other girls. Anyone.'

'Of course not.'

He smiles weakly. 'Thank you,' is all he says.

If there are sad conversations such as this, there is a lot of hilarity too amongst us, a lot of good talk and wit, and there are also silences which bring a sense of quiet understanding to a friendship, enriching it.

The futility of war is never far from being the subject of discussion and I find I return to it myself, as if I am a specialist on the subject, which for good reason I might well be. It seems foolish to imagine that in destroying those things which can not be recreated we will not suffer from the results. And how can the lives of those who have been killed and will continue to be killed be recreated? The gaps they leave will remain gaps forever, and what those men might have contributed to the world in the fields of science, medicine, the arts, in commerce and technology, and in the important area within families, will never be known.

I do not believe now, nor will I ever believe, that even one of those men was meant to die for England or any other country. And that they died gloriously is, to me, a fatuous claim, unworthy of anyone with an iota of intelligence or even common sense.

In these dark moments in my thinking I recall a letter I received from Geoff's special friend, Noel. The two entered air-force camp together, came first and second in their exams in New Zealand and sailed together. Six months after Geoff, an only child, had been killed, his father died — of heartbreak it was clear. I wrote to tell Noel this.

In his reply to my letter Noel wrote:

I was shocked to hear of Mr Chambers' death. What can his wife have to look forward to in life now, with them both gone? It amazes me how such people carry on. Losing the father is sad but to lose anyone as special as Geoff is especially so, and you, Neva, will know even more than I, the attributes Geoff had that put him head and shoulders above anyone else that I, at least, have ever met. I will always remain devastated that he had to be one who hit the deck. His death is an enormous loss to our country. And to you of course. I can't begin to imagine how great that loss is. If I make it, I'll come to Gisborne to see you when this farce is over and we can talk about Geoff, someone who meant so much to each of us.

In contemplating the past, I am grateful that the future comes one day at a time. Life would be unbearable otherwise, if we knew what lay ahead, the miseries to be borne. So I tell myself, take today and deal with it as positively as you can, because life is good for the most part and people are good for the most part. Experience has told me that inward thinking can be destructive and I am pleased to be so busy at times that I am exhausted almost beyond endurance.

Is it tiredness that does something odd to me? I work part of the way into lunchtime and then run along the road to our mess. While negotiating the brick edging of a garden to pass through the gap in the hedge between our two buildings, I catch a foot on a brick and dive into the concrete wall of a garage. For a moment I am stunned and sit swearing. Inside the mess I feel a little different from usual, eat lunch, and am hurrying to clean my teeth when I find myself in a heap half way up the stairs. My nose is bleeding slightly. Back on the footpath by our headquarters building I slide to the ground again.

Later, when I take a NEWZMIL cipher message from London to the colonel in 'Q', he says, 'What's the matter, girl? You look queer and your eyes are bloodshot.'

'I dived into our concrete garage and hit my head,' I say. 'Tripped when I was rushing.'

Indicating a chair and looking very serious, the colonel says, 'Sit down there.'

'I have these other ciphers to take around.'

As if he were training a dog, the colonel points. 'Sit,' he says. I sit. 'Eat this,' he says, handing me an orange. 'It won't hold the war up if those messages don't get delivered for 10 minutes. Use your brain, girl. You have concussion.'

'Have I?'

'You have, and you'd better take it easy for a few days. No excitement, no cartwheels.'

'There's a lump the size of an egg on my head. Feel it.'

Colonels don't usually feel my head, but now this colonel does, watching me intently. 'You'll live,' he says.

For the next few days I feel strange and fall over occasionally without knowing it, confused for a moment after picking myself up and feeling remote from the world. The colonel drops into my office every few hours to make sure I am all right and speaks sternly about taking care of myself — I don't want to end up some sort of gormless idiot, do I? He frightens me and I behave myself, work more slowly, sit very still often, breathe deeply, and go to bed early.

So CONCERNED FOR me is the colonel from 'Q' that he arranges that I have two days in Florence. I am to travel in a YMCA vehicle as far as Fano where an English doctor will organise something from then on. On my appearance at his clinic the doctor leaves a half-clad soldier on a chair, saying 'I'll be back in five minutes,' and escorts me to a three-ton mail truck. Climbing up onto the sacks of mail, I sit alongside three American nurses and a Belgian man who readily reveals that he has been married three times and is about to repeat the performance with what will be Wife Number Four. He is so weird we girls soon realise why each of his marriages has been brief, and we edge away from the sack on which he is sitting. As we drive, I spare a thought for the squashed correspondence some of the forces are about to receive.

There is something more urgent to consider. We need to find a *gabinetto*, a toilet, in the first large town we reach. But in Italy toilets are hard to come by, so we make our way to the hospital where a minute man carrying brooms and buckets escorts us to a fine bathroom complex, opens the door, allows us to pass, then follows us inside.

One of the American girls takes him by the shoulders. 'Hey, you funny little guy,' she says, 'come right on in,' and she pushes him out the door. She turns then to me. 'So you come from Noo Zealand where all those animals are. Tell me, honey, how many faucets has a cow got?'

At our club in Florence, the manager is not very pleased to see me. He tells me I can have a room, but if a soldier wants it I'll have to give it up.

'Fair enough,' I say, but apparently no bedless soldier arrives.

In the morning I go with two officers to the top of the hill to see the Church of San Miniato and the graveyard. Through the grills on the vaults we admire valuable vases, exquisite lace and priceless picture frames, followed constantly by a suspicious monk. To make sure we don't steal a mosaic or piddle in a font, one of the officers says.

On this still bright summer day we then visit the cameo factory and watch a craftsman working on a brooch in the way he has for the past 40 years. He is using shell, he explains, although he sometimes uses mother o' pearl from Australia, and New Zealand is across the harbour bridge from Sydney, isn't it? Finished cameos are priced up to the equivalent of 12 pounds, and thinking of the 12 shillings a day I am now paid, I determine to save every single cigarette and every slab of Patriotic chocolate towards my next visit to Florence.

Instead of staying a second night in Florence I travel to Leghorn with a Kiwi officer, who takes me to the Allied Officers' Club there for dinner and a dance. I am to stay the night at a hostel where a group of ENSA players are billeted, sharing a room with a girl called Sally. When I arrive I can see no sign of her, and searching the rooms find myself in a dormitory with six snoring males. One moves, so I wake him and together we locate Sally on the other side of a locked bedroom door. She is reluctant to open up because she has had a man climb in the window earlier in the evening and has hermetically sealed herself in. When we knock on the door she screams, but once she recognises my voice as perhaps not belonging to her male intruder, she lets me squeeze through a slender slit.

In the morning the Kiwi officer takes me in his jeep to Viaréggio on the coast. The road is lined with trees and seats and shrubs and would be magnificent were it not for the legacy of destruction left by mining and bombing. A prisoner-of-war cage is located here and the PW Command of the 92nd Battalion occupy the most handsome building in the town. The battalion comprises mostly Negroes and I listen to two having an argument. One says, 'Yo-all can't push that down my throat. Ah knows.'

We drive on to Forte de Marmi and further north again, to a point six kilometres south of the Fifth Army front, at the start of a long straight out-of-bounds stretch of road the Germans are watching night and day. Here we lunch to the accompaniment of guns firing and the ground shaking, alarmed to see small children running across the mined land. In our poor Italian we hold a conversation with a boy of about four, and soon afterwards a large Negro saunters across to us. 'Can yo-all understand what that liddle boy is saying?' he wants to know.

We return through the mountains to Lucca, which is large and clean and only slightly damaged, and drive entirely around the road constructed on top of the wall encircling the city.

Back in Leghorn we go to dinner at a prisoner-of-war repatriation unit where the Italian Countess of Fossimbrone is also a guest. The friendship between her and the New Zealand officer in charge of the unit is obviously more than casual.

Before Florence fell, this lady was at a farm buying eggs when two men in British uniforms arrived, asking for vino. The farmer refused to give them any and they swore at him — in German, which the countess recognised. She told the farmer to give the men as much vino as they wanted and she would pay for it. Then she rode off on her bicycle and reported them to the authorities.

The New Zealand officer has taught her to say 'Damn', 'Hell' and 'Just the job' in English. She deserves better.

23

C H A P T E R

WHAT MAIL! I am swamped with it, 14 inter-unit letters, 12 from New Zealand, two from England, and one from my father's sister in County Down. Nothing from Jock. I search through the pile of envelopes again. No, nothing.

A note from my sister, Brownie, is reassuring. I have told her about my engagement to Jock but sworn her to secrecy as far as our parents are concerned. In my letter I wrote:

> *Please promise me that you won't mention this to Mum and Dad. You remember how they suffered when Geoff was killed, not only for me but because he was like a son to them. If I tell them about Jock and anything goes wrong with him they will suffer again, and I couldn't bear that. You can imagine their devastation if your Bill had been killed instead of being taken prisoner. They would have grieved for you as they have for me and I'd like to spare them any more possible unhappiness. Do you recall what Dad said when Geoff went missing and we were waiting for more news? 'We must hope for the best but be prepared for the worst.' That's what I'm hoping for with Jock.*

Brownie replies:

> *Neva, I promise, truly. But I'm so happy for you and hope to God Jock comes through all this bloodiness. You've had enough to contend with. I can't tell you how much I admire you for protecting Mum and Dad when you must be bursting to tell them your good news. Do send a photo of Jock and I'll keep it at work where Mum and Dad won't see it, waiting for the moment you tell me I can show it to them.*

A week later I have a letter from Jock, including photos taken inside the Abbaye du Parc at Louvain. There are general views of the abbey and others of the cloister and the sanctuary, of the dormitory and the library and the refectory. From his Queens Own Cameron Highlander 49th RHU he waxes lyrical about paintings by Reubens and the plaster work on the ceilings in the dining room and library, and trusts that the folder arrives intact. Nothing about what is happening to him and nothing about us. We might be two strangers.

Conversely the Gumboot Canadian writes from up north enclosing a poem:

Of all the things that I yet miss
Most keen — your lovely evening kiss;
And all the war that I yet face
Weighs less than loss of your embrace.

This is a great surprise to me, as the writer has never spoken romantically, although in retrospect I remember that his eyes soften as he pecks me briefly before saying goodbye. Does he mean what he writes and is too shy to express what he feels in person? Or is writing such poems merely relief from wartime tension, something he might send to anyone?

In amongst the mail is another fond offering, this one from a gentle English officer who organised concerts on board ship as we crossed the Mediterranean. Although we seldom met, we had a special rapport. He writes:

M'cushla, I am going home. I am delirious with delight, but there is one regret, Neva, and it is a very real one, that it won't be possible to bid you goodbye personally. I would have given much for that 'sweet sorrow', so my leave-taking will have to be read not heard, and if my words are halting and my phrases clumsy, you will know that it is because my heart is full and there is a lump in my throat.

No words can describe my feelings for you, Neva, and I'm not even going to try to define that loving friendship that has grown up between us. Suffice it to say that it is very beautiful and has given me comforting joy at a time when things were difficult. But what is really more important is that such a friendship can not die, and though the seven seas divide us physically, yet my heart will always beat a little faster with each remembrance of you.

This letter is not going to be a long one, dear, because ordinary news will be out of place in it. I am going down to No. 3 Transit Camp at Naples for a week so, if you could, drop me a line at that address. I would love to hear from you before I go.

And now, darling Neva, farewell. May God bless you and protect you always and carry you back home soon. My thoughts will often be with you, dear, and all my memories will be very sweetly tender. Give my fond regards to Nan, but for yourself, m'cushla, there will always be a part of my heart. I am softly singing 'Haere Ra' as I bid you farewell.

Do we all have beautiful thoughts such as these, and if we do, why do we stifle them, seldom expressing what is lovely and memorable and precious? More especially, why is it that some who have not uttered one word of devotion in person pen me words of indescribable beauty and closeness while Jock, so full of affection when here, tells me at length about the ceiling in an abbey in Belgium? But I do not judge, nor do I compare. In a new field of battle he has more important things with which to occupy his mind.

I forego taking a leave day and write letter after letter after letter, 10 pages home, eight to Geoff's mother, and shorter ones to Vera and Rhoda and Marie and Bobbie and Lorna and Bernie and Bill C. and Bill H. and Bill McC. and Charlie and Bruce and Jim and Ewan and John. Most are inter-unit letters eagerly awaited.

In the morning more mail arrives from Jock. He hopes the abbey photographs arrived safely and tells me the monks grow their own tobacco, that train services where he is are not disrupted as they are here, that the Belgian civilians are on army rations, and that he loves me very much.

I write to him immediately, expressing relief at hearing from him, feeling an urgency as my pen moves across the page, because I have no trust in tomorrows.

Two days later another letter comes from him. His brother in the air force has been severely wounded and has been repatriated with what looks like a broken back. Would I mind writing to his parents? I write to the Schofields, hoping my words are what they want to hear, the sort of letter I am becoming expert at framing, wishing each was unnecessary.

IN THE MORNING we entertain Mr Jordan, the New Zealand High Commissioner in London. Rather, he entertains us. An official photographer is with him, and an RAF officer, plus an army officer who repeats, 'Mr Jordan, we must go now' so often Mr Jordan threatens to change his staff. Mr Jordan tells us of an Orangeman and a Catholic he spoke to in Belfast. The Orangeman said Ireland would be a fine country to live in if it weren't for the Catholics, and the Catholic said he'd enjoy life immensely if all the Protestants were drowned. An eavesdropping bystander added, 'Mr Jordan, faith an' that's how it is. If we were all atheists we could live together like Christians.'

Soon afterwards, on the 12th of July, 1945, Orangeman's Day, I walk into Statistics where Charlie a Protestant and Peg a Catholic work harmoniously side by side most of the time. But on this special day Charlie has tied orange ribbons to the spacebar of Peg's typewriter, to the handles of filing cabinets and to the legs of her chair.

When I enter the room Charlie winks at me, but Peg does not look up from her machine. Later she tells me she is so hurt and angry she will never speak to Charlie again. She does, but not until Charlie has been persuaded to apologise, no doubt with his tongue in his cheek. Two otherwise mild people behaving like this! What hope for Northern Ireland?

Another visitor we host is Sir Patrick Duff, the newly-appointed United Kingdom High Commissioner in New Zealand, ready to take over from Sir Harry Batterbee. Three high-ranking officers are with him. We are not sure why these people have been brought to meet us but do our best to be pleasant. Bob the cook excels himself, providing oyster patties which melt in the mouth, though Sir Patrick expresses dismay when he can not find an oyster in his. One of his party, who has been on duty in Canada, tells us that the American girls are lovely but have no brains. However, he supposes they are good for the morale, adding that they are for his. I wonder what salary these men are paid.

A huge pile of parcels has just arrived. Two for me hold pyjamas made by Mum and Auntie May, there are biscuits from friends of Mum and Dad, Geoff's mother sends sweets, a cake and biscuits, and his Dunedin aunt sends more biscuits. I wish that in the same mail a letter from Brownie had not been written on 5 March, the third anniversary of the day Geoff was posted missing. Despite the parcels I am suddenly empty of feeling.

24

*O*UR WESTERN FRONT has extended to 20 kilometres and Germany is allowing convoys from Switzerland to come in for prisoners. Surely this will mean to the Oflag where Brownie's Bill is. Even German policemen are fighting in Berlin now. And our army is pushing on, moving forward every 20 or 30 minutes. Montgomery says a quick result depends on supplies, and surely this can be solved. It is wonderful to think that the end could be very close, but as I have so often thought, nerve-wracking to consider what might happen between now and then. Oh, and our Prime Minister has announced that after this our men will see Burma and the Pacific through! When will it really and truly ever end?

The Kiwi Concert Party is in town. Their concert is uplifting, lots of fine singing and dancing, clever and amusing skits, and producer Terry Vaughan plays the piano with a scarf draped along the keyboard. We feel affection for the female impersonators who wear our mosquito nets in one item. After much comedy and clapping, the response to a female impersonator's 'Ave Maria' brings the house down. Surely that tells us how much the soldiers appreciate quality rather than smut, which is what many other concert parties offer.

I speak to two brothers who are members of the concert party. Tears fall freely as they tell me of a third brother, also a member of the concert party, who was killed when visiting a relative in the Maori Battalion. Their anger towards the Germans is frightening if understandable.

Shaking talcum powder over myself today I think of Italy's smells. Apart from those of dirt and engines, they are almost non-existent. Even the violets and geraniums and jonquils in our mess gardens have no perfume. If you were blind, they could be lumps of wood.

And if it is true that the birds have been eaten, I want to know how they were all caught? It would be difficult to catch every bird in the country, wouldn't it? Were I a bird I would quickly fly to one of the highest twigs in the land, well out of harm's way. And I wouldn't sing a note for fear of being discovered. Perhaps that is what has happened. Perhaps the foliage of the cypresses and the oleanders is filled with silent feathered friends, but they would not perch in the arthritic olives with their inhospitable bare gnarled branches.

Although it is fine now, it has been raining heavily. As the roof of my office leaks I sit at my desk wearing gumboots, and because the air is humid I have opened the window wide and also the French doors. The sergeant-major from Ciphers negotiates the puddles on the floor by walking on his heels and when he enters the room a sudden gust of wind lifts a message marked 'Top Secret' off my desk and carries it out through the window.

Together the sergeant-major and I stifle our laughter as we watch it lift and fall, lift and fall, before settling on a *casa* rooftop. Then I look at the sergeant-major and he looks at me.

'I know,' he says, 'I'll have to get the bloody thing.'

'That's how it looks,' I say.

Off he goes to find a ladder as I stand watching to see if the cipher blows off the roof. But it behaves and the sergeant-major's quest is successful, and all is well.

Amongst another deluge of mail which has arrived, Mum says that dental nurse Brownie, who has been transferred to the air force station at Whenuapai, is at home on leave and having nightmares, and that Dad is much better. Better than what she does not say. No one has told me he has been unwell and I worry that they are hiding something from me in the way that I hide things from them.

And a friend writes that the rationing is severe, that it is a struggle to make do with the amount of butter and meat allowed, and of course her car is up on blocks and she has to walk everywhere or go by taxi or bus. I put her letter on the bottom of those waiting to be answered.

A moving note arrives from Jock. He is about to go into action and is writing 'just in case'. I think of the letter about rationing, pick it up intending to tear it up, then return it to its place. I forgive my friend for not having any imagination. It isn't her fault, I suppose, but I'm not sure. It makes me dread going home.

A sergeant takes me to a dance at the YMCA Leave Hostel at Riccione. Nan comes too, although she despises dancing and thinks it a waste of time. The sergeant is possessive but a superb dancer and we wish the floor was entirely ours. A soldier talking to Nan tells her the sergeant is my 'steady', which I didn't know.

BRIGADIER STEVENS SUMMONS me to his room to say he has had a call from the officer commanding the Palestinian Arab Unit. They are to be stationed for a short time here in Senigállia and our girls must be very careful, especially Miss Morrison. In my mind I dream up an *8th Army News* article — 'Body of New Zealand servicewoman discovered near canal. Head rammed in. Size 11 footprints found nearby, plus one New Zealand shoulder title.' I could rival Jane on the back page. But the memories which crowd my mind are not amusing. I see a ploughed field, feel hands groping at me, a huge penis poking, and a knife at my forehead. A shiver passes through me.

Our boys are again in battle. The volume of stuff going north is terrific. Last night there were sounds like shelling or bombing quite close to us and the villa shook. Trains are groaning past day and night with supplies, and the air is a constant whirr of aircraft on their way to cause destruction. I stood on the balcony and watched wave upon wave go over and thought of Geoff, and of a lovely Australian pilot who is with No.3 Squadron, imagining him on one of their sorties and wondering if he would come back. Deep down inside I am infuriated, it is all so awful I can't bear it, can't bear it. I am filled with a desperation I am not altogether sure I can handle.

What I need at exactly that moment arrives unexpectedly — 'call me Cliff', so gentle and kind always. He takes me for a drive to Mondolfo, then inland on Route 16. American ammunition dumps and an airfield have been blown up and are ablaze with light. The area is a hive of busyness as hundreds of trucks come and go incessantly. The Allies now have the use of every aircraft in the Central Mediterranean Forces and the Middle East, a change from the usual cry for air support. Two American bombers, despite their instruments, radio beams, FDL smoke screens, et cetera, have dropped several loads behind the lines. One of them fell amongst Kiwis, with no casualties fortunately; another fell on Poles, killing 45, a damned disgrace.

To cross a river our men have six bridges up in two hours and with flame-throwers mow down everything on the opposite bank. The 21st Battalion have quite heavy casualties but the Maori Battalion reach their objective without one man being killed.

And down south an ammunition ship in Bari harbour has blown up. Every living soul on the docks has been killed or wounded — 3000 casualties, 1000 dead. Men sitting at a meal table had flesh blown off their bodies and boots have been found with tangled bones in them. Doors and windows miles away have been flung across rooms and become embedded in walls opposite. Oh, my God!

In Naples the Germans have dropped two bombs in the harbour. The sky is lit up over the sea near us and we can hear rifle shots. And President Roosevelt is dead.

German prisoners of war are being sent south in closed cattle trucks. It is awful to see their faces as they crane their heads up to the slits of windows near the top. How dare mankind be as brutal as it is, how dare it kill and maim? And how dare it crush men up in cattle trucks as if they are animals? Oh, I know these particular men are the enemy. I know that. But it is all wrong, wrong, wrong.

On and on it goes. Some of us climb the stairs to the rooftop at 4.30 this morning when we hear loud explosions. The sky is aglow and smoke rolls thick and fast in our direction, the glare increasing with each explosion. And lying in bed on the balcony I look up at the sky, which is moonless. Raking across it are criss-crossing Allied searchlights. Will they find what they are looking for, an enemy reconnaissance aircraft?

In need of a kind of healing, perhaps, and because it is there, four of us go into Ancona to hear a Welsh choir, which is magic. They sing Welsh songs as you'd expect, but also Scottish, English, Irish and American. Towards the end of the concert the pianist plays songs with the tune disguised and we have to guess what the songs are. The audience on the side of the theatre which fails to guess has to sing the tune. On his sixth attempt a naval officer up in the gods guesses correctly and is made to sing solo. In a magnificent baritone he thrills us all with 'Oh, It's Quiet Down Here' and gets a standing ovation.

We go, too, to a symphony concert at the Garrison Theatre, and hear the music of Rossini and Delibes, Puccini and Leoncavallo, Liszt and Mozart, Ponchielli and Handel, Gounod and Tchaikovsky. Nothing can mar the peace which is mine.

NEXT DAY IS my twenty-fifth birthday and off and on the sergeant-major from Ciphers brings me greetings cables from New Zealand. On his last visit he does not leave but simply stands after handing me the message, watching closely.

'I just love birthdays,' I say, and I open the envelope eagerly. I am very happy.

The message from Jock's sister reads: 'Sorry to tell you Jock killed 20 April. Writing. Love. Betty Schofield.'

I can not speak. Gulping and stunned, I am barely aware that the sergeant-major is holding me tightly in his arms. I think he is making cooing sounds.

25
CHAPTER

I DON'T KNOW what to do as my eyes fill with tears and my throat becomes rigid. I am in some sort of suspended animation and don't care what happens to me. Anyone could cut me with a knife or stick needles into me and I would not feel them.

The sergeant-major is still holding me and although I am aware that he is speaking, for a time I have no notion what he is saying, then I hear the words, 'I'm sorry, Neva. I'm so sorry.'

When he leaves I take hold of myself. I long for Mum and Dad, wish I could lean against the strength which is my father but he is a long way away. With an aching throat I sit at my desk. My hand shakes as I reach for a register. In columns I write words and figures with my fountain pen and put blue and pink and white forms in piles, mopping up my relentless tears with blotting paper.

Then for a time I lean against the window frame looking out over the rooftops, thinking of Jock's tall figure, seeing his gentle smile, remembering his thoughtfulness towards me always. Married to him I would have felt safe, and God knows that is what I want, to feel safe and at peace. Despite my hesitancy in uttering the word 'Yes' to him, I had been grateful to Jock for his certainty about our future together, was banking on it. And now, 'What future?' my mind wants to know. He was too lovely to die.

Vaguely I notice that there is not a vestige of cloud in the sky and that the air is not breathing. The day's peacefulness is somehow a thorn in my side. I turn away. Closing my office door I sit at my desk, pull a register towards me, pick up my fountain pen and begin again to enter words and figures in columns. My throat is an iron bar and my eyes overflow.

At dinner I tell the girls about Jock. They all make the right noises and hug and kiss me. They care, I am sure of that, and I love them so much I could burst. Looking at them I try to smile, knowing that although they are sad on my behalf, they have no real understanding of what has happened, which is not their fault. They have not been where I am now.

Dot arrives from Egypt on an official visit and although she is sympathetic and understands that I would prefer to be alone there is no way I can avoid accompanying her and two very senior officers to a South African concert, which is apparently very good. I see nothing of it because the moment the theatre lights go out tears roll down my cheeks and I think of Jock. When I hear clapping I clap, although what it is I am clapping for I don't know. Tennyson would have said I was moaning when Jock put out to sea.

I feel crushed, listening but not feeling as more news comes in. Benito Mussolini has been caught by Partisans while trying to escape to Switzerland and has been shot, hung or executed. We are told that his body is in Milan's main square where Fascists recently executed 17 of their enemy countrymen. All day long thousands of Italians stream by to view their erstwhile leader's body and fire a volley of bullets into it. The three Italian girls at our mess are crying with joy.

Our Main Division has lost contact with the Rear Division and no one can find the brigades, the troops are advancing so rapidly. The German's strongest fort, near Venice, is expected to fall shortly. Munich has fallen, Berlin is a city of the dead, and the Russians are giving the enemy hell. Dreadful stories are coming through of German atrocities, and deputations of British Government members have crossed the Channel to observe and judge. And Goering has either resigned or committed suicide. It is difficult to know what is true and what is not with so much news flying hither and thither, some of it confusing. We do know positively that the Germans in Italy have unconditionally surrendered. Another thing we know is that we have taken over the magnificent Danieli Hotel in Venice as our New Zealand Club there. Immediately Venice fell General Freyberg sent officers into the city to take over the hotel which he knew well from peacetime days.

The sergeant-major from Ciphers asks me to his office for coffee. He says he wants to tell me that he knows what I am suffering. This man, with whom I have shared so much good talk, has never before revealed what it is that makes him somehow special and now I know.

This is what he tells me. When he sailed for overseas he was married and his wife was pregnant. One night after his arrival in Italy a message came through from Army Headquarters in Wellington, 'Please tell Sgt-Major M. his wife has died in childbirth.'

'I was on duty and took the message,' the sergeant-major says. His gentle brown eyes water and then he smiles. 'My son's nearly two. He's with my mother.' From a battle-dress pocket he brings out a photograph of an appealing small blonde boy asleep, using a large yellow collie dog as a pillow.

'Shouldn't you go home?' I ask.

'Gary's being well cared for, and how can I go home when so many guys are still being killed? I'll stay here until it's all over, and then I'll be the happiest bloke alive.'

AT 9 A.M. ON 8 May 1945, 18 days after Jock is killed, there is a special victory church service. The programme is headed 'Order of Service on the Occasion of the Cessation of Hostilities'. I am deputed to sit on the stage representing our Clerical Division WAACs, a lone female in a row of senior officers. Our lovely chaplain, Reverend G.A.D. Spence, calls us to worship, announces the hymns and has us pray.

My mind wanders from what is happening because if it stays on the service I will cry, feeling I've not a lot to thank God for. To rein myself in, as it were, I count the heads of the soldiers in the front row, then the feet, then examine how the men are sitting, feet together, apart, or legs crossed. This fills in time, and certainly when the others on stage look sombre as is appropriate, I too look sombre for a reason of my own.

When Reverend Spence asks us all to join him in a special prayer our collective voices echo around the walls in a kind of murmured dirge.

Before Almighty God we declare together that as we have striven in war, so, with
His help, shall we strive even more mightily in peace:
To bring a sense of dignity and worth to every member of the human race.
To treat with reverence, as a trust, all things of earth and sky and sea.
To put away all hatred, bearing one another's burdens.
To offer in His service the skills and products of hand and brain in industry and
art and education.
To assume our full share of responsibility in the family of nations.
To be born anew in the Spirit, that a new world may come to pass in which every
nation and people may have just opportunity.

And before the Blessing we again pray:

Eternal God, the Father of all mankind, we commit to thee the needs of the world. Where there is hatred, give love; where there is injury, pardon; where there is distrust, faith; where there is despair, hope; where there is darkness, light; through Jesus Christ our Saviour and Redeemer.

It is almost too much to expect of God, I think, and far too much to expect of me. A large part of my love has been destroyed and I am filled with enormous distrust and a sense of injury and despair. Life has robbed and battered and cheated me. How can I do what is expected of me when I feel so angry and so useless?

The service over, I can not speak to anyone on stage and walk off alone into the mass of soldiers as they leave the hall, intending to join the other girls. But the Ciphers sergeant-major appears from nowhere and takes my arm.

'You need a drink,' he says. Holding hands we walk together to his quarters where he momentarily disappears while I sit on the concrete steps and wait. Soon he emerges with a small bottle of *vino rosso* and two glasses.

'Before I pour it . . . ,' he says, and when I look at him, wondering what he means, he lifts my chin and kisses me on the lips. I feel myself breaking into pieces and I sob into his battle-dress jacket. Then he opens the bottle.

26

WORK GOES ON as it must. Before too long we will move to Florence, so in an attempt to increase our finances, Nan and Maurine and I go to the lovely Coronaldo area with a provost and three others, taking articles to sell to an Italian family the men know well. We reason that accompanied by a provost we shouldn't get into too much trouble if we are caught.

We drive into a farmyard and tumble into a large warm kitchen where a smiling young housewife cooks us 18 eggs and shows us photographs of her husband, now a prisoner of war in Germany. We admire his good looks and the good looks of her baby which Nan and I each nurse briefly, making tutting noises. I sell a pair of grey flannel slacks for 1200 lire, the equivalent of three pounds, a khaki skirt for 1000 lire, and a sleeveless Patriotic jumper for 600 lire. Overall this young wife and her wizened old father spend a great deal of money, but as they have a lot of lire and little clothing, their purchases please them as much as they do us.

Young Fabio is home again from Naval College and the guards have handed me two letters and a magnificent bunch of roses from him. He is looking more and more handsome, I notice, as I call from the balcony to thank him when I see him passing later. His smile is quite brilliant as he looks up and pleads with me once again not to read his letters 'at my friends'. And then he mouths the word 'I-T-A-L-Y', 'I Trust and Love You'.

There are victory parties going on in all of the messes, and as everyone is dropping in on everyone else, the hilarity is overwhelming.

In contrast to all the craziness brought on by relief at the war news, Jock's photo arrives from his sister Betty. It was taken in England before he left for Belgium, and he looks so wholesome in his kilt. I hold it for a long time, a cardboard replica of what was real flesh and blood. Jock, I say, you are a really nice person. Was, that should be of course. Of course. You must be realistic.

There are moments I can't believe he is dead, and with his photo in my hands, this is one of them.

Brownie writes that after hearing of Jock's death she lay awake all night crying, which makes me pleased Mum and Dad know nothing of it. I find it difficult to put on paper how I myself feel. It's as if my emotions are at the bottom of a pit too deep to plumb, and physically I feel anaesthetised, unable even to imagine my father saying 'We're here, Nugget' as he had said when Geoff was killed. This time I am quite alone.

I read Brownie's letter again before tucking myself into bed on the balcony. The padre across the road stands looking up at me. Am I ill, he asks. I tell him 'No, I am fine, thank you,' and he goes away. Then I cry myself to sleep.

NEXT MORNING I have something else to occupy my mind. Recently a girl I shall call S. took late leave without asking for it. And last night another girl woke me to say her bed was missing, which I can not believe, but it is true. I organise the guards to find a replacement, which they do, and at breakfast ask the girls if they know anything about a missing bed. With no hesitation S. says, 'I gave it to my friend and he took it round to 'C' mess.' Sensing something more serious than what I am hearing, I say no more, but later I call S. to my office.

'You know you can't give our beds to anyone, don't you?' I say.

'My friend needed a bed and I gave him one,' S. answers airily.

'Never do it again then.'

'Okay,' she says, just as airily.

The friend she means is a Scot, engaged to a girl back home, but S. has a ardent New Zealander admirer too. I am very confused when S. says she is going to marry the Scot and is sending home to her mother for a special ring.

First I speak to her Kiwi friend who says he is in love with S. and has asked her to marry him. Then I speak to the Scot who says he knows nothing of his marrying S. He likes her very much, but that is all — it is his fiancee he loves.

Next day a message comes from a little lacemaker in the village, claiming that S. owes her thousands of dollars. Again I call S. to my office.

'How much do you owe this lady?' I ask.

'Nothing,' S. says. 'She's a dirty, filthy liar.'

I consult our Director of Medical Services, who has S. hospitalised, and we take up a collection and pay her debt to the lacemaker.

At the hospital S. escapes from her bed and runs along the beach naked, so is sent to a British psychiatric centre to the north. When I visit her she pleads with me not to let her room-mate near her, saying she loathes her, which is quite untrue. They have always been particularly close.

Several times I see S. and on each visit I consult the chief psychiatrist, a skinny little man with eyes which bore right through you. He recommends that S. be sent home.

I tell S. and she laughs and laughs. 'He's mad,' she says. And just before I leave she whispers, 'Next time you come, will you bring me a long needle? I can frighten them with that.' As I walk away, her laughter rings out.

27

CHAPTER

*O*UR CAMP COMMANDANT had reason to reprimand a soldier for drunkenness and received this note in reply:

> *Sir,*
> *I have to inform you of results obtained from the informal lecture given me last Saturday re intoxicating liquors and consumption thereof. This practice has ceased, a feat of which I am justly proud. The only liquor consumed by me in the last three days has been six glasses of red wine and my beer issue, plus one bottle of beer presented to myself by another soldier for services rendered, repairing of watches, pocket. In lieu of drinking, I have taken up table tennis, and the practising of harps, Jewish, as soon as one becomes available. Hoping this report meets with your approval. I have the honour to be, Sir,*
> *Your obedient servant,*
> *C.M. 450905*

The Camp Commandant considers taking up the Jew's-harp appropriate for this soldier, because with the amount of alcohol he is consuming he is rapidly heading for heaven where he might find a use for it — unless he goes somewhere else.

BECAUSE NAN AND I no longer work in the same office we have been able to take Venice leave together. We travel in a New Zealand truck, and as usual find locating toilets a difficulty so we visit what was the Polish hospital, now an Italian dispensary. En route a notice beside two Bailey bridges tells us they are the 'Two Types', named after the pukka English officer duo in the *8th Army News* cartoons. By the approaches to another bridge is a large sign: 'This bridge took a bloody long time to build. Watch your spacing.'

The countryside is as bleak as expected, with war debris and deserted villages, until we reach lovely wooded areas. Ten hours after leaving our mess we are at Mairena where a New Zealand rest camp is located, only 30 kilometres south of Venice. Each morning a truck takes our boys from the camp into the city and brings them back at midnight. The camp was occupied previously by the Germans and is quite beautiful, the large buildings and a host of tents softened by elegant trees, yet still not a bird sound. Not a single tweet.

Why did I imagine gondolas to be brightly painted instead of what they are, black, with drab and dirtyish gondoliers? Along the Grand Canal we are taken, while other craft enter or leave smaller canals as their gondoliers manoeuvre them with expertise. At the Danieli Hotel, our New Zealand Club, we linger over deep hot baths and dry ourselves with towels as large as tablecloths.

Cramming everything possible into our three days' leave Nan and I walk and walk. The sights and sounds of Venice soothe the jagged edges of my thinking and I can even smile to think how much Jock would have enjoyed sharing this as we shared Rome. But Nan is fine company. We admire the exterior of St Mark's church, stand in awe of the clock tower and the bell-ringers and the horses in the Square and smile at the innocence of tiny children feeding the pigeons, we ponder over the sadness of the Bridge of Sighs and lean from the top of the steps on the Rialto Bridge to watch a funeral procession of gondolas pass by quietly. Not a sound of a motor on the canals. Just peace.

In the twilight we have a slow and tranquil excursion down the Grand Canal with four New Zealanders from the club. I think Nan almost succumbs to the romance of the occasion, and I most willingly do. It seems I am enveloped in a blanket of beauty I want to bottle up like a precious perfume, so later I can remove the cork, inhale, and relive the experience all over again, see and feel the wonder, the peace and the company. I say, 'I wish the gondolier would lose his way and not be able to find the Danieli. I'd like this to go on for ever.' He finds his way of course.

'The magic might not be over,' one of the men says.

'It is for Nan and me. We're off to Milan in the morning.'

'That's not what I mean.'

As I step from the gondola this soldier takes my hand. His face is indistinct in the fading light, but his touch is not. Many men have touched my hand, including the lovely Jock, but without the strange stirring I am aware of now, and while the feeling excites me it brings with it a slight fear. I must not read too much into it, must not trust my emotions. Too much has been stolen from me.

Besides which, this is Venice and I am intoxicated by its magnificence and uniqueness. Want to be intoxicated.

Yet, 'The magic might not be over,' the soldier says with a smile in his voice, and I like that. His name is Tony.

'I'm going to call you Tone,' I say.

'I don't suppose I can stop you doing that.'

'No.'

'I'll call you Neve, then.'

'That's fine by me.'

In bed I think about his using the word 'magic'. Words are important to me. In my mind I store the right ones away as I will his perfect 'magic', but I will recall it in context. Venice, magic, Tone, in that order. Or should it be Venice, Tone, magic? Given time I'll work that out.

In retrospect the trip to Milan is an error of judgement. Had we previously met the mad major with the jeep Nan and I would have walked. He drives so fast we wonder whether we will ever make the almost 450 kilometres and he seems incapable of travelling for more than half an hour without stopping for a drink. By the time we reach Milan he is driving on the wrong side of the road, scraping trees and Italian carts, and terrifying men on bicycles. As the landscape passes by in a blur, he even negotiates an occasional footpath. When he stops at traffic lights in the centre of Milan we leap out, saying 'Thank you so much', and find our way to the Officers' Transit Hotel.

In the lounge we meet a New Zealander who says he will arrange a flight back to Venice if we come to the airport in the morning.

The next morning we enjoy a swim in the seaplane lagoon, take some photographs, and lunch in what the pilots call their hotel. Then news comes. The aircraft is out of oil, there will be a hold-up. Oil arrives, but of the wrong type. It is now 3.30 p.m. and we have to be back in Venice tonight in order to catch our transport to Senigállia in the morning. Feeling responsible and panic-stricken, the New Zealander drives us onto the main road to hitchhike.

In short bursts, we travel 50 kilometres in a variety of vehicles until a young soldier with a jeep picks us up and takes us to Cassana, but unfortunately he has his girlfriend with him and has no desire to drive at anything but a snail's pace. At Cassana his commanding officer lends us a vehicle and driver to get us to Brescia. As no transport whatever comes along there, the driver asks an American provost for more petrol and we are on the road once more.

Stopping for a coffee we are delighted to find a driver going to Verona, so swop over into his vehicle, and reach the town as light is fading. Our driver is determined to take us on to Venice because hitching after dark is too dangerous, but first he must go to his headquarters 30 kilometres off the main highway to say goodbye to his commanding officer, who is leaving at dawn. Nan and I sit outside the headquarters by the lovely Lake Forlinini while the necessary goodbyes are said, and then we all set off for Venice. It is 11 p.m.

The four-hour drive is uneventful, but arriving in Venice at 3 a.m. presents further difficulties as the gondola service ceases at midnight. There is nothing our driver can do but depart, and Nan and I set off to walk feeling apprehensive, as we have no notion how to find the Danieli.

Perhaps the boy does this every night. Where he comes from we don't know, but he emerges from the darkness and says he will take us by a short cut. He is about 10 years old. He runs off saying 'Come', and with no alternative we run after him. We weave through Venice, behind and in front of tall buildings, by canals and nowhere near canals, we dodge through archways, we cross bridge after bridge, some stepped, some not, hardly caring that we might be knifed in the dark. Then we suddenly see St Mark's Square and feel safe and grateful and exhausted. Our relief is so great we pay the boy more than we can afford. He quickly melts into the darkness and we tuck ourselves inside the Danieli. We wish we had never gone to Milan.

BACK AT SENIGÁLLIA I look in the mirror and see a slightly different person from the one who left here. I wear a relieved expression and my eyes look clearer. Deep down little has changed, but my reflection tells me nothing of that. I am ready for work again.

Four letters await me, their timing all wrong. One is from Jock's father, one is from his sister, and two are from Jock himself. Reading them depletes every ounce of my newly found energy. I weep at Mr Schofield's description of Jock's fine work prospects, of his school and university records, what friends thought of him, and the huge gap he will leave within the family. Betty's letter encloses a note a padre found in a pocket of Jock's uniform after he was killed. 'Neva, a more charming person one could not wish to meet anywhere, but, alas, I shall see her no more.' This brings a deluge of tears. Betty writes that Jock told the family his mind was firmly made up, that he was moving to New Zealand when the war was over and he and I would take up the threads where we had left them.

Painfully reading each word on each page of Jock's two letters I imagine him choosing his phrases with care and affection, and I want to know exactly how he was killed, if others were with him, and if so, who they were. I want to know where he is buried, where his bones lie. And I want, with a kind of desperation, to know if his body was identifiable, or, like Geoff's, not so. A huge ache rolls around my body like a cloud, and for some reason I feel extraordinarily heavy.

When Geoff was killed my father told me I would survive because I'd be able to and I had to, and now I would have to do that all over again. Geoff's death taught me that suffering brings an incalculable richness, just as a wonderful perfume can be produced by crushing a beautiful flower and destroying it, but right now I am by no means ready to consider this truth. I want to shout, 'It isn't fair, God.'

Slowly, after Geoff's death, I learned, too, that what happens to you is not as important as what you do with what happens to you. The wisdom of this does not stop me from feeling totally alone here in the midst of so many, nor does it stop me longing for my father's shoulder and his voice and his smile. Tired of fighting to be a survivor, I am on the verge of giving up. It is such hard work.

28
CHAPTER

SOMEONE GIVES ME a copy of what he calls a very free translation of a captured German document:

> *Dear NSV*, you've all we need,*
> *A pipe to smoke, a fragrant weed*
> *To puff at in one's hour of leisure,*
> *Art photos for our sensual pleasure,*
> *A concertina we can squeeze,*
> *Figs, dates and plums straight off the trees,*
> *And songs to sing and songs to shout;*
> *The so-refreshing acid drop,*
> *And buttons if your trousers pop;*
> *Crosswords for brains as sharp as flint.*
> *In short, the lot — but niente bint,*
> *Haven't you something in the shop*
> *With curves that know just when to stop?*
> *But not some aged shop storekeeper.*
> *'Twould only make our rage the deeper.*
> *Year in, year out, you send away*
> *The mothers and the kids to stay,*
> *And this you term evacuation,*
> *While here we lack all stimulation.*
> *Doesn't the framework of your scheme*
> *Envisage sending a harem*
> *To frontline folk for their selection,*
> *Indulging each man's predilection?*
> *Oh, what a party that would be!*

So help us please, dear NSV
Yours sincerely,
Fieldpost Number X
*NSV — Nazionalsozialistische Volksgemeinschaft, the Nazi Party Comrades Association.

Then followed the reply:

My dear old Fieldpost Number X,
The idea's great, but lay off sex.
If everybody wants to mate
Who's going to do guards on the gate?
Perish the thought! Don't dwell on that.
Many would leave their sweeties flat,
And mount — just ponder on this trifle —
With babes in arms in lieu of rifle.
Moreover, all you guys impassioned,
Just bear in mind that girls are rationed.
The only ones that don't need points
Are aged aunts with creaking joints
Mustachioed like a sergeant-major.
Purge your emotions. You'll be sager
Till you come out on leave with zest
Or better still, if not the best,
Till Churchill's laid at last to rest.
Then when war at last is won
And you come home, for everyone
There'll be a merry, laughing bride
To build and share your nest with pride.
And lastly — this should make you happy —
NSV supplies the nappy.

OUR ITALIAN MAIDS must be getting tired, or perhaps only confident. Their housekeeping is appalling and I've had to speak firmly to Marcella, which isn't easy because she makes me want to laugh. She speaks to us in a mixture of Italian and English and emphasises dramatically, as if we are all mentally deficient. This is accompanied by an exaggerated use of hand and arm gestures and an incredible variety of facial expressions. The combination makes it difficult to take her seriously.

When I make a complaint she puts down her iron. Of course, signorina, she understands, but while she herself is working little Gina sits in the sun instead of cleaning the floors; but she is so young, perhaps I do not realise that. And yes, everywhere there is dust which normally Rena chases away with her dusters and polish; but poor Rena, she is so worried about her *marito* who might be dead, signorina, and her *bambino* is sick and her mother fell in the drain while beating her washing against the stones and is *molto doloro*.

Marcella's exquisite concern changes suddenly. She smiles so her teeth shine and assures me that she will *parlare* with both girls and she is *dispiace*, signorina; it will never happen again. She picks up her iron. I am dismissed.

I have a strange dream and hope it is meaningless. In my dream I dress and leave the hotel at which I am staying and go for a walk. Along the footpath I meet Central Registry's corporal, whom I consistently dodge when I am awake. We decide to walk together into the country. Tiring, we sit on the side of the road and go to sleep. I am wakened by someone tipping two tiny black and white puppies on my head. The man who does this is large and repulsive, unwashed, unshaven, and frightening. The corporal and I run from him towards Sydney. I have promised a Sydney RAF pilot that I will phone him if ever I am in his city, so I say to the corporal, 'I must find a telephone,' and we run faster.

After a long time we see two telephone booths in the distance but I realise I've no money.

'Have you any pennies?' I ask the corporal.

'Yes,' he says, 'but you'll have to repay me.'

Both booths are out of order, so off we run again and have not gone far when I wake with a start.

Finding myself in my bed on the balcony I smile. How like the corporal to want his pennies back.

I make one last visit to S. She thinks she is going blind and has several other complaints. When she was last examined she told the doctor she heard voices in her head and felt people were in her room when she was alone. She told him, too, that when she was a child she tried to commit suicide, that her sister found her with an iodine bottle in her hand after she had swallowed the contents. She says that in telling the doctor these things, she was so nervous she broke her rosary beads which had been blessed by the Pope. She shows me the beads, which are in three pieces. The psychiatrist has taken her scissors from her, she says, because he is afraid she will attempt suicide again.

With a wide smile she adds, 'I give them awful frights.' Then she begins to sing in a loud voice and all the other patients in the lounge stare at her.

I GO WITH a Gisborne soldier to see a documentary made on the visit of the British Members of Parliament to German prison camps. We see the ovens in which bodies were burnt and living skeletons, barely able to walk, and others lying among the dead waiting for death to claim them too. Some lie perfectly still and others writhe in agony. It is shocking to watch and I have to force myself to remain in the theatre. I want to know the truth and, God help us, this is true.

Three Gisborne boys ask me up to the Riccione Hostel where they are part of a Leadership Group. When I admire a beautiful scarf one soldier is wearing, he says he would not part with it for a thousand pounds as it was given to him by a girl in Trieste who was shot soon afterwards for speaking to Kiwis.

I speak to a Yugoslav there too. He studied engineering in England before the war and until the cessation of hostilities was in the Yugoslav Air Force. Now he is attached to the RAF. I am very engrossed in what he is telling me when one of our men whispers to me that the Yugoslav was wearing a hairnet when he arrived. On this he is judged, and for this reason, it seems, I should cease speaking to him.

It is so hot hell must have the heat turned up. In the night there has been one of Italy's sudden storms but the sea is tranquil when Thel and I swim during siesta. We are sunbathing happily when a young man runs gasping along the sand and asks us to help find the body of an Italian boy drowned yesterday morning in a storm.

With some reservations we join two Kiwis on a *mosconi*, Thelma with her hands over her eyes lest she see the body. An Italian policeman has been searching for some time exactly where the boy went missing and, although he has found nothing, still he paddles in circles in the transparent water barely half a metre deep. Thinking him quite crazy, we venture into deeper water, reasoning that the body will not have remained in one spot during a storm.

A shriek rents the air. It is Thel's. 'I-th-think I s-saw it.'

A fisherman joins us flourishing what looks like a butterfly net, and we think he must be crazy too, but after a glance into the water, he puts his net away, picks up a rod with a huge hook on the end of it, loops this into the boy's bathing trunks and drags the body ashore.

Eavesdropping, we learn that the doctor had forbidden the young epileptic to enter the water, but ignoring this, and in a storm, the boy had gone out alone on a *mosconi*. The craft had no sides, and with its seats high in the air on two floats, it provided no protection whatever against his toppling into the water when he had a fit. Even worse, he could not swim.

OUR EX-OC, DOT, is over from Egypt again, about to do a little 'swanning' up north. We have a good sing-song at 'A' mess — lovely songs, 'My Beautiful Sarie Marais', 'Isle of Capri', 'Return to Sorrento' and, of course, 'You Are My Sunshine'. And Brigadier Stevens makes me sing my silly 'All the Little Pansy Faces' with my toes turned in, as I did in a concert when I was in Standard 1.

All the little pansy faces
Growing in the garden there,
Look at me with eyes of longing
For I am their lady FAIR.

And when I come out to greet them,
Leaning like a queen above,
All the little pansy faces
Look at me with . . . eyes . . . of . . . L O V E.'

Everyone laughs, which was the brigadier's intention, I suppose. He is so proper it surprises everyone when he shows any levity.

As the wartime activities peter out the crossword puzzle craze overtakes Headquarters. I enter the military secretary's office where he sits head down and wearing a worried expression, as if the fate of the New Zealand Division depended on him. Slowly he raises his head and deeply intones, 'A fat bird files a petition. Seven letters.'

Our troops have been withdrawn to Spoleto from Trieste, where they were having a riotous time apparently. Rumour tells us that 99 percent of the girls in Trieste are merely highly educated prostitutes and that their mothers, whose husbands are away, are worse. Our VD figures are alarmingly high, and one decorated officer is said to have set up his own brothel.

We had a two-man German submarine washed up on our beach recently, and last week when a group of us were swimming we found a strange head bobbing amongst us. It belonged to a dead German.

DROVES OF MEN are going home. At 8.30 this morning we all go down to Camp Headquarters to say goodbye to 10 truckloads going to Advanced Base, and I've never seen so many wrecks and black eyes in my life. The 'marrieds' will go home immediately and there will be a ballot for the 'singles'. What a day for them all. No one could have visualised that the war would drag on for the time it has and no one would dare pass judgement on a wreck, with or without a black eye.

The most momentous news is that a second atomic bomb has been dropped on Japan and the Japanese have agreed to surrender provided their Emperor is not touched. Any news we get from that area comes through American radio interception.

It is ironical that on VJ Day I receive two letters of mine written to Jock, each stamped 'We regret that the contents of this package were unable to be delivered, the reason being that the addressee is deceased.' I suppose this is a peacetime stamp used by all post offices, but in wartime surely the message could be less painfully worded.

All round us parties go on, but I am not missed when I go to bed early with the two letters under my pillow.

29
CHAPTER

MAIL COMES ERRATICALLY, and when it does arrive there are mountains of it. From home we often used the special airgraph forms available. On these the name and address of the recipient was printed (never typed) in block letters in a marked out area and you then wrote your one-page effort. Black ink was recommended or a 'B' pencil, and very small writing frowned upon. As if we were all some special brand of wartime morons, it was then explained to us in writing that we must affix a stamp in the space provided and take the form to the post office where it would be dealt with! If for any unfathomable reason you preferred to, you could send your form direct to the airgraph office at Wellington's General Post Office, in which case the form was to be folded as few times as possible parallel with the lines of writing.

Now on the other end of such messages, I know the magic of the process. I open a small windowed envelope marked 'Airgraph Message'. Inside it is a page measuring approximately 12 by 10 centimetres, a numbered miniature photographic negative of the original message. This method of lessening the space needed for transporting mail to the forces is a triumph of technology and I wonder who dreamt it up.

Apart from mail from New Zealand, the quantity of inter-unit mail I get is massive, and as receiving letters is so important to the men I slog along writing brief notes to dozens. Not one of the men writes letters such as Geoff wrote. From his pen and in his beautiful handwriting flowed the most unusual, intelligent and wondrous prose about anything at all. He was the most articulate of men.

All these letters and day by day experiences bring a sense of growing to my being, and I realise that I am changing at the same time as being constant in many ways. This is confusing because, while my level of tolerance has increased, conversely I am much more sceptical than I was and certainly I am much more angry at times. Consequently there is a constant battle to achieve a workable balance of emotions. It would be easier not to bother indulging in the painful business of examining the inner workings of your mind, but I do, and of one thing I'm quite certain. I'm learning a hell of a lot about a hell of a lot.

Many of our units are out of action at the moment, thank heaven. There is still a lot of talk about the terrible waste at Cassino, as there always will be perhaps, about the Maori Battalion's valiant fighting around the railway station, and of the terrible loss of life of others in our Division, including some who — together with Indians — were climbing up the rock face. In that one battle at Cassino we lost 2000 young lives. For nothing! Personal stories filter through of the lack of animosity between the common German soldiers and ours, and of the unbelievable experience of some sharing adjoining rooms in an Italian house with the enemy, with both groups emerging next day ready to kill each other. Doesn't that tell you everything you need to know about the futility of what is happening? No wonder there is a lot of anger and disillusionment about.

The military secretary, from whom I get most of my Divisional news, tells me that the four day supply of food with which a Russian soldier is issued is equal to an English soldier's rations for one day. Also, that the Russians are very young and quite untrained. Each is given arms, carries two shells under his arm, and joins the thousands who go forward to wipe out everything in their path, they hope. Or be wiped out.

Right now Mr Churchill and others are at the Yalta Conference on the Black Sea, and sadly two aircraft carrying English members to the conference have crashed.

Some of our Headquarters folk are packing up to go home, and others call in from the Division to say goodbye, most of them with a bottle of something in their hand. Even after we have gone to bed some arrive, so we put our greatcoats on over our pyjamas, have one drink with them and slink back to our rooms again.

Flying thick and fast are signals and ciphers I must deal with, and there are mess canteen accounts to straighten out, and also I must do an inventory of all of our clothing.

Some of us go to the concert, sitting amongst men ready to go home. An Englishman nearby must have been sorely affected by the war, I think. He wears silver-rimmed glasses and mumbles 'What rubbish,' 'How awful' and 'Why on earth is he allowed on the stage?' And out of tune he whistles any song he recognises. His moroseness is overwhelming, yet when the band strikes up 'In the

Mood' he leaps to his feet, claps, shouts, and stamps his feet. 'Hot diggety-dog,' he shrieks. I'm pleased he is not a Kiwi.

Some of the girls are shivering after injections, which seem a never-ending business. They can barely smile when the Quartermaster chief calls to question Bob the cook, who sold all the blankets off our beds when we were at work yesterday. Bob is something of a mystery. He tells us he will never be welcome back on his West Coast. What exactly this means he doesn't say, but we assume his selling our blankets is a sympton of whatever criminal disease it is he suffers from.

30

*T*ONE IS ON leave after sitting at the hospital watching life ebb from his brother, badly wounded on the last day of battle. On the beach he tells me of the wounds and what it was like sitting by his brother's hospital bed, hoping without hope, and listening as each breath became fainter.

Looking out to sea, I tell him about Geoff and Jock and my devastation and anger.

'In Venice I thought you were the happiest girl I'd ever met.'

'We spend a lot of time pretending, don't we?'

'It's sometimes the only thing to do. And because you pretend and because you smile and then for a moment don't, someone will say, "What's the matter with you?" What makes it worse is that it's always the glum-bums who ask such inane questions.' Tone looks glum himself.

'You're a kindred spirit.' As I speak, I feel a little like Anne of Green Gables.

While Tone is here, we talk as we sit on the beach, we swim, we eat scones with raspberry jam on them at the English YMCA, and we see *Tosca* and *La Bohème*.

We walk country roads in the fading twilight, marvelling at the fireflies and the tracery of the trees against the sky, pausing to listen to Italian voices arguing or singing or laughing.

One walk takes us past the grave of a solitary German soldier. On a narrow winding track edged with tall trees whose branches meet above our heads, we stop and read the name on the small white cross, Helmut Schmidt, and the age, 18 years. As we stand in silent sympathy an ancient farmer wearing ragged grey trousers, a black shirt and a cap stops beside us, points to the cross and shakes his head, then walks on. He is carrying a turkey.

Still looking at the cross, Tone says, 'Poor bastard. And I suppose his family will never know where he's buried.'

I think of Geoff, one of three air crew unable to be identified, buried in a military cemetery at Benghazi. And I think of Jock, buried where? Even if logic says it doesn't matter I want to know. I tell Tone and from then on he holds my hand as we walk, and I am glad, pressing my fingers hard into his palm.

Wherever we go I am aware of his strong presence, physical of course, but also mental and spiritual; I feel like I've been washed up on a gentle emotional shore. Thinking of him when we are apart makes me smile. It's a long time since I've felt this way. Whole. Is that any sort of way to describe yourself? Whole?

One day we take a picnic lunch to wherever our feet lead us. In my satchel I take sandwiches made by Bob, a tin of pineapple, four oranges and a book of Rupert Brooke's poems. Tone takes chocolate, beer and a slender volume of verses entitled *A Soldier's Spare-time Soliloquy*, written by a New Zealander attached to Fourth Field Ambulance.

Edging the canal we stride out in our shorts past old men playing their finger game — *due, tre*, et cetera — waving as they pause to call 'Bella gamba, signorina' and 'Inamorata!', meaning 'Beautiful legs, signorina' and 'Sweetheart'. Walking on we hear their laughter and then 'tre, quattro, cinque'.

We stop to tell a boy leading two white, long-horned oxen how magnificent his animals are, and his cheeky black dog barks at us. On a small arched bridge spanning a stream a boy and girl are kissing, the bunch of white flowers the girl is holding stark against the man's dark jacket.

Beyond a small farmhouse built hard against a hill we find a path leading to a stream. Along this we walk, passing two drunken haystacks, one large, one small.

'Mother and child,' Tone says.

A farmer's wife carrying a baby stands on the path watching her chickens peck at the dirt. Her skirt touches the ground, her dark blouse hangs untidily from one shoulder and around her head she wears a red and white spotted handkerchief. The baby wears nothing.

We find what we think the perfect spot, a glade by the bank of a stream, with trees for shade and a panorama of flat land on the other shore where a steep-roofed stone farmhouse with one doorway and two very high small windows seems to be growing out of the earth. The fence around the house is made of long thin sticks nailed or tied closely together. We think we see a small boy watching us from outside the gateway.

On the ground we spread a khaki blanket off my bed, and Tone says, 'I'll put the tins in the stream to keep them cold.'

'And I'll put the sandwiches in the shade so they don't shrivel up — unless you like eating cardboard, Tone.'

'I'm trying to give it up,' he says.

We have a swim before eating, and as we emerge the figure we imagined we saw by the farmyard fence appears, a small boy as we thought, all in grey. Without a word he passes us, returning with a sheep and riding it across a shallow section of the stream. Over and over again he repeats this until he looks at us and says, 'Finito.' We clap and Tone gives him an orange.

I unpack the food and laugh. 'The choice of sandwich is spam or spam. Which would you like?'

'I think I'll have spam.'

'I wonder why.'

After eating the slightly curled sandwiches and tinned pineapple we lie and read.

'How do you feel about ideals?' Tone asks after a while. 'This guy's strong on them.'

'Too many dissolve into nothing.'

'But we must have them, Neve. Something to strive towards, something keeping us on the straight and narrow.'

'Who wants to be there?'

'What about on the comparatively straight and narrow then?'

'That's better.'

'Seriously, this bloke has ideals I admire, and values I like — loyalty and steadfastness and tolerance and charity.'

'I'm all for those. I'll bet he has a lovely Mum.'

'What about a lovely Dad?'

'Sure. I have the loveliest father in the entire universe, have I told you that?'

'Mine's pretty good.'

'To have a son like you, he has to be all right.'

'The value I like most is loyalty,' says Tone.

'Me too.' I like the way our conversation is going, light, a little teasing, but uncomplicated. Safe, you could say.

We read on. I don't like Rupert Brooke's 'The Soldier'. At this time I'm not into some corner of a foreign field being forever England because the bones of a perfectly good airman or soldier like Geoff or Jock have been poked into a hole there. And the line 'In that rich dust a richer dust concealed' disturbs me because the richer dust shouldn't even be there. Wouldn't be there if all Tone's idealism worked. I want very much to explain this to him but it's too involved and I'm too hot and lazy. Some other time.

Geoff used to quote Brooke's sonnet, 'Oh, Death will find me, Long before I tire of watching you,' imagining his getting to heaven before me and watching me arrive, a 'most individual and bewildering ghost' turning and tossing my 'brown delightful head amusedly, among the ancient Dead'. Goodbye, Geoff, my one huge love, and goodbye all those praiseworthy ideals. All I want is kindness and understanding.

This is what I tell myself often, but is it true, I wonder? Is this really all I want? A small voice says there must be more, there is definitely more, but I am afraid to listen.

I turn a page and read about things Rupert Brooke loved, white plates and cups, clean-gleaming, ringed with blue lines; and feathery faery dust; wet roofs beneath the lamplight; the strong crusts of friendly bread — oh, I like that.

'Why are you smiling?' asks Tone.

'I thought you were reading.'

'Why are you smiling?'

'I'm smiling at the line "the strong crusts of friendly bread". It beats patriotic stuff hands down.'

'In your opinion.'

I look at Tone. 'Do you find me intolerant?' I am earnest.

'I find you hurt.'

'You're hurt too. Tell me you understand.'

'No one understands more. And I'm as angry as hell.'

'This bloody war, Tone!'

'And there's not a thing we can do except live through it. You're good for me, Neve, you know that?'

'You're good for me too, and I'm going to cry.'

'I'll get that last can out of the stream, and we'll drink to propping each other up.'

We drink our beer and Tone tells me about his family in Christchurch and his victim-of-the-bottle Uncle Perce who embarrasses them every Christmas by telling lewd jokes, whose values are purely alcoholic. And I tell him about a relative-by-marriage who came to Gisborne on holiday when I was small and always brought dressing-up things for kids, although she was about 30, ancient anyway, and unmarried. I tell about the ditties she taught us and how my sister and cousins and I loved them but Mum and Dad didn't. I say the one we were regularly implored not to sing was 'It's not so much the fish as the parsley round the dish that tickles the old man's nose'. 'None of us knew what it meant, and I'm still not sure.'

Tone puts back his head and laughs and laughs, then leaning at an angle, turns and faces me. 'You're the funniest girl,' he says. And he falls into the stream.

31
CHAPTER

*A*LETTER FROM home tells me that Brownie's Bill is back in Gisborne, but that she is still up at Whenuapai in the Air Force and isn't allowed leave unless to be married. Well, she is to be married, but not the day her fiance arrives back in the country a walking skeleton. He needs to be fattened up and must make some decisions about their future before the wedding march is played. I can't believe the air force can be so rigid towards the fiancee of a first echelon soldier, one of 'the red blood of Gisborne' as the local newspaper put it, and one who has been a POW since Alamein. How much more inhumanity does he have to tolerate, and why isn't the rule about leave broken, for heaven's sake? We were told that nothing was going to be too good for men like Bill. Were the powers-that-be aware of the ambiguity of that statement?

A leave centre has been organised up in the Dolomites and I'm arranging a leave roster. I'm to go almost immediately, and Nan will accompany me.

The night before we leave one of the guards is drunk on duty and even more abusive than he is when sober, so I see the camp commandant and the guard is to be discharged. My sympathy for a soldier ceases when we are abused for no reason other than that we are female and we are here, and if this man feels as he does, obviously being a guard at a WAAC mess is the wrong place for him.

Nan and I travel on the back of a YMCA truck, and we stay at the Riccione Hostel for the night, in such quietness we can't sleep. With a speedster at the wheel we rollick on to Venice in the morning, scraping one truck and ripping the canopy off another.

Via Vicenza and Verona, the following day we drive up the eastern side of the vivid blue Lake Garda, where the mountain peaks are snow-covered and on the steep hills quaint Austrian and Tyrolean houses gather like friends.

If I were the fainting type, I would have dropped to the ground at the sight of Madonna Campiglio Leave Centre. We have three *albergos* and can play tennis, swim in a large freezing-cold pool, play golf, tramp and rock-climb.

In the village we buy lace, and scenes and animals carved out of wood. Prices are exorbitant, but the soap and cigarettes and chocolate we brought with us work admirably. Dinner is accompanied by an orchestra, and we discover that the pianist is married to the accordionist who, in partnership with the violinist, keeps a stationery shop in the village. We find this amusing for a reason I can't explain. It might be the thin air at this height.

Next morning, action. We drive along a jeep track for five kilometres and then tramp up a steep path through pine forest to begin with, then over open grassy country, and finally across rocky terrain. And there is the Tuckett Hut, a young *albergo* itself, looking like a Christmas card! The building is of grey slab stone and the cosy inside is lined with plain knotted pine. We fall hot and exhausted onto seats around long dining tables and drink six cups of tea each — the usual, we are assured.

As it is still very light, we don oversized deep blue German alpine suits and large boots in readiness for a rock-climbing lesson. The rock face is six metres high, straight up and down, and we are to climb it. On a single rope we obey instructions, always keeping three points on the rock, two feet and a hand, or two hands and a foot. We understand when one of our men freezes part of the way to the top, his fear so great he can not hear the guides telling him to relax. He will be gently lowered.

The guides tell us that some visitors can't sleep at this height, and others have trouble breathing — as did Peter McIntyre, our official war artist, who gasped all night and had to be hurried back to Madonna early in the morning.

As we walk back to the *albergo*, a guide walking in front of me turns. 'Tomorrow you will come to the top with me.' He is looking up at the mighty Castelletto Inferiore, 2364 metres high, dark and sinister.

'Certainly not,' I say.

'First we will go to another rock school and after lunch we will climb it,' says the guide.

For between one and two hours we tramp to the site of the second rock school for another practice. In the huge and heavy boots my feet feel like houses. Dragging this weight Nan and I climb to within 25 metres of the top of the rock before changing into felt-soled shoes three sizes too large. There is no alternative. Up and down, up and down we go. Oh, the bliss of abseiling on a double rope, sitting in the air and leaping backwards in huge bounds, kicking against the rock and leaping, kicking and leaping, going down, down, down. By now we are firm friends with our guides. Nan's Raphael is 38, an ex-lieutenant in the Alpine Army. My Giglio is 28. Both speak passable English, learnt from the Kiwis over the past few months.

After lunch at Tuckett Hutt we take off for the ascent of Castelletto Inferiore. As we climb with single ropes Nan and Raphael are sometimes above my guide and me, and sometimes we are above them. When we wait for the other two to change over for the first time, Giglio tells me he has shrapnel in both eyes after serving in the army.

'Already I am learning Braille,' he says.

'You're going blind?'

'In a few years, the doctor says. So I am ready.'

'You're being so cheerful about it.'

'What else should I do?'

Up and up we climb, on the outside of the perpendicular rockface and up chimneys barely wide enough to squeeze through. Each time we pause on what the guides call a jeep track, as wide as a foot, Giglio gives me a wee hug and says, 'Come, we will go.'

Together on the crest of the mountain Nan and I walk the last metre of rock, a still perilously narrow 'jeep track'. Our guides undo a tin chained to the summit, take out the visitors' book and show us the signatures of famous climbers of a variety of nationalities who have been there before us. We add our names to the list and smile as our names are bracketed and the words 'First New Zealand ladies' printed alongside them.

After abseiling down the rock we tramp back to Tuckett Hut which looks like a matchbox. Looking up at the giant which is Castelletto Inferiore, Nan and I think that to have climbed it we must be brain damaged.

A small celebration takes place to mark the event and we are presented with a silver cup each — a stemmed wine glass covered with tinfoil.

After dinner we sit around the tables singing and being shown Italian tricks, all strangely feeble, most finishing with a glass of water being tipped over someone's head or down someone's trousers.

Back at Madonna di Campiglio we play tennis and badminton all the following day and this brings up blood blisters on the soles of Nan's feet. The Regimental Aid Post at the *albergo* is in a bathroom, where Nan is dealt with by a doctor full of brandy he has been given after laying out the body of a young Italian boy in the village. As he and Nan use the toilet as an ashtray he tells her she is bloody foolish, and asks what she thinks he can do with feet like hers. She tells him she is more interested in discovering what she herself can do with feet like hers. He carries on smoking and drinking brandy, telling us at the same time that although Cleopatra was beautiful her breath reeked and she had lousy teeth, and that the story of Adam and Eve and the apple is untrue. The truth is that they were a green pair. As if on demand, we smile.

Nan can't swim because her feet must be kept dry, so we go horse-riding in the village on mountain ponies, which object to moving on flat terrain. In the evening we listen to wonderful violin music and I fall in love with a tune called 'Chiesetta Alpina' ('Little Church in the Mountains'). We sleep then beneath true eiderdowns weighing nothing and measuring a foot in thickness, and waken to the sound of cowbells.

We are meant to stay another night here but change plans, our driver being willing. After a night back in Venice we set off for Klagenfurt, and because our driver likes picking up hitchhikers, we soon have a league of nations on the back of the truck. North of Udine we add air force men from South Africa, Australia and England. Then we pick up a small Scot stationed nearby. He is allowed to cross the border at any time to see his Austrian fräulein and always takes his rifle with him because SS troops are still in the hills we are passing. He is serving in a unit whose job is to capture these Germans, and he is quite upset because he has not shot one for three days.

At Klagenfurt we have a cup of tea at the NAAFI (the Navy, Army and Air Force Institutes' canteen) and drive back towards the border. At Udine the petrol point is closed according to a sign at the gate, but the officer in charge sneaks us through and gives us 24 gallons. We smile at a second sign which reads:

NOSMO
KING

which we assume means we must not smoke.

On we rush, hoping this time to arrive back in Venice before the gondolas cease running at midnight.

32

*B*USY IN A crazy sort of way, I squeeze in organising inoculations for us all, and also boots as close to the right size as possible for the girls going up to Madonna Campiglio. From experience I know it isn't easy to find a minute niche in a rock when your toe is nowhere near the end of your boot, and it's a bit dangerous to rely on faith, but it seems there has never been a soldier with a foot size of less than 10.

Three senior Welfare Division girls from Cairo are to be housed with us briefly before going on what they tell us is a buying trip in Northern Italy for the Cairo, Bari and Rome clubs. They are, they say, on a tour of duty but I call it something else. It seems extraordinary if not incredible that it is necessary to purchase anything for even one club at the tail end of the war. And are three girls needed? Couldn't two do the job? Or one?

Courts-martial are being held here and there and two of our girls are working on these in Rome and Bologna. Others have flu. One has been in hospital with something glandular and another is there looking very pale and rickety with her second bout of trench mouth, and yet another has sprained an ankle.

What is worse is that Min is becoming very dreamy and strange. She has taken to putting sticking plaster at the top of her nose and at the sides of her eyes, to avoid getting wrinkles. It is all grotesque, something I can't understand, and it is very worrying. Tonight she was late for dinner and I called at her room to find her between tears and ethereal bliss reading Shakespeare. When I asked if she felt all right she said she didn't know, which is alarming in itself. From what we know nothing major has occurred in her life, but our emotions have been overworked and obviously something is going wrong inside our lovely Min's mind. I have a word with her boss at the Medical Office, and he says he'll keep a close eye on her.

Hurrah! Brownie and her Bill were married last Saturday. But in her letter giving me this news, my mother says she won't tell me about the wedding because

Brownie will want to do so herself. Brownie writes that it was a happy occasion but she won't tell me about it because Mum will want to. And Dad writes to say he doesn't like weddings so will leave describing Brownie's to someone else.

One of our guards regularly reads his Bible as he protects us from danger. I lend him my Rupert Brooke volume and he surprises me by returning it with a note saying his favourite poems are 'The Great Lover' and 'Thoughts on the Shape of the Human Body'.

The little tailor next door has been dealing with the shape of my human body, making me a new dress uniform, a pair of slacks and two pairs of shorts for 3000 lire. Two provosts have just sold all my chocolate and cigarettes and I have a credit of almost 4000 lire, but rather than money, the tailor and his ever-smiling Semolina prefer clothing. I take them a battle-dress blouse, a skirt, a cardigan which has never fitted properly and a pair of army pyjamas, and they react as though they have won a lottery. When I then produce six of the 15 cakes of soap and one of the six tubes of toothpaste Mum recently sent and press these upon them, the tailor wipes tears from his eyes and in sympathy Semolina stops smiling and sniffs. Perhaps discomfited too, the pair of hens on the windowsill cackle as though each has laid an egg and hop to the ground.

Two of our girls are very upset. Thel, who had become engaged, is bereft because on his return to New Zealand her fiance visited his ex-wife who had run off with an American in Wellington. The American has been killed in the Pacific Islands and Thel's fiance is terribly sorry but he has remarried his wife.

Another girl who was engaged before leaving home has been concerned for a long time, knowing that her fiance was a POW in Japanese hands. Today she hears from home that he is back in New Zealand as thin as a rake handle and mentally disturbed. She is very quiet.

At a minor level, Marcella is weeping all over the mess. Sobbing, she confesses that she left a lot of our washing on the line overnight and most of it has been stolen. She is so *dispiace*, signorina, that she can't smile, and our camp commandant can't smile either when I report to him each girl's loss. He says that from now till we move north the Italians will steal anything not nailed down and wants to know what sort of blasted fool Marcella was to leave the stuff on the line. I can't answer that.

The brigadier has gone up to Florence to make decisions about our moving there, and a few of us smarten up our stockings in preparation for that exciting event. We dye one pair of grey stockings from the officers' shop with Condy's

Crystals and another pair with a solution made from our mepachrine tablets, intended for mosquito protection but also found useful as a suntan lotion. The mepachrine solution wins hands down, so we dye three pairs of stockings each.

In the village I see a blue angora twin set which I feel it imperative to possess. It is priced at the equivalent of less than £19, which I don't have as I've spent my credit, so I review my wardrobe before sending Marcella into the neighbourhood with underwear, cosmetics and, of course, soap and cigarettes and chocolate. By the end of the day I am in credit to the right amount. For her bother I present Marcella with a pair of shoes, and she in gratitude presents me with two metres of heavenly pink lace.

Fabio sends me a bunch of lovely zinnias, each bloom perfumed, imagine! He's strong on perfume, and perfume is strong on him, overpowering in fact.

I go to Florence to see what our accommodation at the Minerva Hotel will be. A colonel picks me up in his staff car and less than five hours later we are in the City of Flowers, Firenze.

With Brigadier Stevens and six colonels I have a very stiff lunch in General Freyberg's lounge, being careful that no word of mine can be construed as being frivolous. I think some of the colonels are doing the same thing, and this is confirmed when one winks at me surreptiously over the dessert. I wink back.

With this group I go then to the Minerva where we have a meeting and make decisions. Today the Americans leave the hotel and tomorrow we take it over complete with 55 Italian staff, including interpreters. Five of the staff comprise one family, the proprietress being one of them. A most charming creature, she claims to be a friend of the Queen of England, and is quick to relate that she has stayed at the residence of the Duke of Connaught.

There are two beautiful lounges in the hotel and the mess rooms on the same floor are as lovely. Our 'A' mess officers will eat in splendid isolation, 'B' and 'C' officers will dine together, and we girls will be by ourselves. The room allotted to me is very satisfying. A short stairway off the passage leads to the door. The large bedroom looks over a piazza with trees and gardens and fountains. And no buckets of rusty water here. I have my own bathroom.

BACK AT SENIGÁLLIA I find Tone there. He is on a course but before he returns to his unit we can have one day together. It will be Sunday, the only day I don't work. Without speaking, we know where we will spend that day.

The stream is the same, the trees are the same, even the small boy is the same, but this time he wears a blue shirt rather than a grey. He does not drive sheep today but he walks from his house, crosses the stream and lingers. Tone gives him two oranges.

I've brought with me a library book on art because if we are to be in Florence I want to be more familiar than I am with some of the famous artists.

Tone says he likes the traditionalists, Turner and so on. 'Don't go much for the moderns.'

'What about the Impressionists, with all their colour and big brush strokes?'

'They're better than real with all their liveliness, and I love what they do with people. Which of them do you like?'

I consider this. 'Pissaro and Cezanne and Monet. Oh, and I'm a fan of Lautrec and his naughty prostitutes with their black stockings and ginger hair.'

'You'd make a good Lautrec prostitute.'

'Tone!'

'Well, I can imagine you dancing in black stockings. Maybe not the ginger hair though.'

Tone tells me that Russia has a large collection of the Impressionists and the Germans an even larger collection of Greek sculptures. 'Nations have always taken treasures from other nations and paid little or nothing for them.'

We discuss the appreciation of art and writing, about understanding each more if you study or practise only quality art or quality writing.

I tell Tone about Dad and his constant search for knowledge and never being without reference books around him. 'He chose my name, Neva, after reading of Rasputin and his power over the Russian Royals, when he could have suggested the name of any one of his numerous sisters or at least something Irish, Peggy or Colleen perhaps.'

'No. You are an individual and need a special name. You're no copy of anyone else. You have singular importance. You're unique.'

'I doubt it,' I say. 'Sitting on the top of Castelletto Inferiore, I felt almost as if I didn't exist, and if I didn't it wouldn't matter. From up there everything down below was so minute, so unimportant — and that includes human beings. I didn't feel unique or even vaguely important. Truly it seemed we really don't matter a lot in the scheme of things.'

'You matter to me, Neve.'

I smile. 'I'm glad, because you matter to me too.'

We are lying face down, and he reaches over and puts an arm around me, draws me close and kisses me. The kiss is like a drug I want more of.

'You know I love you, don't you?' Tone says.

'And I love you.'

Tone sits up suddenly and turns away. For what seems a long time he is silent before turning back.

'Neve, I should have told you before. I'm married.'

I gasp and say 'I don't believe it', then I gather my senses. 'Oh, Tone, why didn't you tell me?'

'It didn't matter until I knew I loved you the way I do. I love your mind and your body and your whimsical, amusing ways and your kindness and your common sense. Everything about you I love.' He holds my hand very tightly.

I say, 'And I love you to pieces.'

'I'm sorry, Neve.'

Neither speaks for a time. 'I suppose we'll survive,' I say. I am getting to despise that word. Survive.

'All we can do is practise what we value most — loyalty. If you can do that, so can I, although it'll be bloody difficult.'

I can't reply, and look away at the stream. Then 'I'm never coming here with anyone else,' I say. 'It's where we said we love each other. It's ours.'

When I turn back Tone is holding his head down, with his hands over his face. In silence I wait. He looks at me and smiles such a smile. 'I'll take you with me wherever I go,' he says.

'Yes, sure. That's how it is with me too.'

We kiss, and kiss again. And again. Both our faces are wet.

33

I AM FEELING sorry for myself. There are thistles in the fields of all of our lives, I suppose, but those in mine at the moment seem extra tall. And my memories are clenched knuckle white. The sun doesn't shine as it should, and the attention of men other than Tone is as welcome as a cockroach on my pillow. When I swim with others I am quite alone and when I dive beneath a wave and emerge with a smile on my face I am crying. Oh, yes, all of these things.

Yet life goes on. Work, and listening to men from the Division talk. How they love that. For them we represent home as we speak of people and places and events to which they can relate. It is a long time since they have known anything as close to normalcy as our company. But talk and love are often too quickly enmeshed, and many do not know that their attention can be smothering, even unwelcome. If we are an oasis in the desert to the men, we girls walk a mental tightrope at times. Like S. Like lovely Min.

Men who are demanding put a special burden on us. A sergeant who has pestered me beyond endurance turned sour recently. His attention is exhausting and he has become a nuisance, and I give him as gentle a rebuff as I am able.

'You damn WAACs,' he says. 'You don't get killed.'

'I apologise for that,' I say, but smile, hoping to make him see how ridiculous he is.

'You don't even get wounded.'

'No, we don't,' I answer. 'Please forgive us.'

Now the soldier's lips move towards a smile. 'I'm sorry,' he mutters.

'It's my turn to forgive you,' I tell him, and all is as well as it can be.

When I see Tone again I tell him about this sort of response, and about my one critic amongst the girls.

In his usual sensible way he says, 'If you succeed at what you're doing, someone will always criticise you. In your field you're a proven expert and don't need to apologise to anyone, Neve. And you have two choices — you either ignore the criticism or come out fighting and jump on someone fearlessly. You'll know when to do which, but don't hesitate to jump if you know you're right.'

Such philosophy. No wonder I like him. Correct that. Love him.

I wonder and wonder about Tone. Does he trust his emotions? Perhaps when he goes home he will forget I exist. I don't want to believe this, and inside my head say, *Please don't forget. I won't let you. I'll haunt you, Tone. I really will.*

Why does he have to be married? I decide to take care never to love again, even marry anyone at all, so avoiding being hurt. And I will not be afraid of being alone. Theoretically I am very brave.

Another thought occurs to me. There might be something wonderful waiting around a corner for me and, although I have nothing on which to base such optimism, if that is so I wouldn't like to miss it.

If I've been unlucky, I might be lucky too. Long ago at home I heard my mother say 'Things change,' for what reason I can't recall. Why then, do I remember that as she spoke she was making peanut butter? She had minced the peanuts three times, added the butter one of us had made from our cow's cream in the squared glass churn with the beater beneath its lid, added salt, and there it was, our Mum's delicious peanut butter.

'Things change,' she said.

And Dad added, 'It's the only thing that's constant, change.'

The only thing that is constant is change, I thought, listening. I had imprinted that on my mind because it sounded wise, and clever too. I had no way of knowing then how true it was.

34

W HEN THE TROOPS arrived in Florence close on the heels of the South Africans, children were held up to be kissed, wine was handed to our men, and tanks were bedecked with roses in this City of Flowers. We girls have a less flamboyant entrance, sitting in the back of 15-hundredweight trucks and three-tonners, quite unnoticed by the populace.

We move into the Minerva Hotel. Immediately I am closeted away to discuss Patriotic issues, tailors, laundry, complaints, mess fees, meal hours, office hours, late leave, provosts, et cetera.

In our large office block the brigadier occupies a conference room with a blue and white tiled ensuite bathroom. Most offices look out over wide and busy thoroughfares and rattling trams, but mine is at the rear of the block, and my view is of a quiet courtyard. Only an occasional pedestrian crosses it from time to time.

The brigadier takes me to see where most of our male staff will be billeted — in three huge buildings which are sadly dilapidated but stand in beautiful grounds with paths and gardens and fountains and statuaries.

On a rise nearby is the Villa Bobolini where 2 Echelon and Archives will sleep and eat and work. Pay staff will eat and sleep here too, but will work in the city. A truck service will run all these people into our central offices.

On our first day in our new location there are ructions. The men are furious that we girls have such superior quarters, and more furious because we are there with nothing but officers. They do not hear us when we explain that we do not eat with the officers, and absolutely do not sleep with the officers.

At the men's camp, what is called an indignation meeting has been held and the men affected have been moved to more updated buildings, which they deserve. Nevertheless, for reasons of distance and transport in non-working hours, the most angry of them are sharing accommodation in the city.

A number of men have come to me to complain personally about our superior lodgings. Diplomatic though I try to be, they leave my office sulking. One of the most unpleasant complainants works in Central Registry next to me. In between is my tiny map room which I pass through to reach my own office. After all his insulting language and his criticisms of our girls and myself, this man now asks if his office can take over my map room.

I choose not to be confrontational, not to ask if maybe he is asking a lot after his behaviour. Recalling Tone's advice, I smile widely, and simply say, 'No. Sorry.'

We notice that the men who are grizzling are all recently arrived 15th reinforcements who have seen no action. To a front-line soldier office accommodation is unimportant compared with life and death.

At the Minerva we have a grossly obese porter who speaks little English and dislikes anyone who can. If we ask him a question, in incomprehensible undertones he mutters what sounds like, 'Woggle, woggle.'

I am asleep when the receptionist rings and asks if a tap is running in my bathroom as there is a flood in the basement. With half-closed eyes I inspect the situation and assure her that no tap is running in my bathroom and crawl back into bed.

Immediately there is a knock on my door and, again with half-closed eyes, I answer it. Standing there is the woggle-woggle man. He has come, he says, to inspect my bathroom. Turning sideways he squeezes down the few stairs. I follow him to where he stands staring down into my toilet which has made soft gurgling sounds ever since our arrival. I explain this to the woggle-woggle man who ignores me, flushes the toilet, and leaves the room sideways. There hasn't been a gurgle since. How am I going to face him in the morning?

A tailor works upstairs in the hotel and is making a dressing-gown for me out of two blankets I dyed a strange maroon shade. I fear that after dealing with our American predecessors he might charge alarmingly. During my fitting I am surprised at the time he takes to measure my bust and hips especially, so on further visits I will be accompanied.

United Kingdom leave of 18 days each has begun, and the first three men depart today. I've applied for permits for all of our girls to go, two or four at a time.

A large number of letters arrive today from New Zealand, one of them from Geoff's mother, Sue, who says that as soon as I get home I must marry or I'll be like her, with a walking stick, peppermints and a cat. I suspect this is a sample of what to expect when we go home.

Tone enters the office as I finish reading Sue's warning note, putting a new complexion on my day. We walk across the arched Ponte Santa Trinita and the unique Ponte Vecchio too, charmed by the shops and houses flanking it. We carry on along the corridor above that joins the Uffizi and Pitti Galleries. We drive then to San Miniato and stand looking at the mighty dome of the thirteenth century Santa Maria del Fiore cathedral.

Tone turns and points to little Fiesele in the distance with the Appenines behind it. 'That's where I could live.'

'We have nothing like it at home, have we?' I say. 'We haven't the architects or craftsmen the old cultures had.'

'Our pioneers were too busy chopping down trees to develop farms and build homes to indulge in frills,' Tone says. 'We should be proud of what we've achieved in a short time.' He takes my hand in his. 'When we get home we'll think New Zealand isn't too bad a place to be. You'll see.'

I am too contented to think otherwise.

'And don't forget the patronage of the Catholic church here,' Tone reminds me.

As we talk the twilight ends without warning. Night pulls a sudden blind down over the city and lights begin to twinkle.

'Magic again,' Tone says, and kisses me. I feel I have no clothes on but want him to go on kissing me.

I know exactly why he suddenly draws away with a soft sigh. He still holds my hand though. Very hard.

Solemnly then we watch the lights below, scarcely aware any longer of the beauty before us. It seems masochistic madness, yet right in an excruciating sort of way, that two people in love should be so determinedly loyal to someone half a world away.

35

CHAPTER

'ANY IDEA WHEN you'll be going home?' We are sitting in Tone's jeep on a cloudless still night.

'I'm a coward. Not ready to face the inane things people will say to me or expect of me. I've told the brigadier I'd like to stay behind with the Rear Party, so that's what I'm doing.'

Tone touches my shoulder. 'What have I done to you? You deserve happiness, not this.'

'I've had such happiness too, Tone. Don't forget that.'

'It's trite to say no one can take from us what we have, but it's true — something special and unforgettable. I'll always treasure it.'

I look directly at him. 'Do you really and truly and God's honour mean that, Tone? That you'll always treasure what we've known?'

'Cross my heart. Listen. I can't bear to think of a future without you, or think of you spending your life with someone else. Can you hear me, my love? I want you to remember that, wherever you are and wherever I am. For ever. Print it on your mind. Take it with you wherever you go always. Promise me.'

'I promise.'

We are silent for a long, long time before moving to safer ground. Tone tells me of a forthcoming rugby match in which he will play in a position not his own, where he knows he won't be wildly successful, and I say the thing I miss in Florence is the superb swimming we had in Senigállia. I tell him how we stood deep in the water with our feet astride playing whales, the front one dog-paddling through the tunnel of legs, then the next one and so on.

'Typical of whales of course,' says Tone. I can feel him smiling in the dark.

There are other smiles. When using a Florentine tram we discover that you get on at the rear and off at the front. At each stop we do what others do, gradually push forward. The six seats on the tram are occupied by Italian men, and as one becomes vacant, another man is ready to dart for it. The rest of us stand, mothers with babies on their hips, women with bundles of shopping resting on their feet, old men and old ladies, and people like ourselves. Slowly we make our way towards the front of the tram through a host of garlic-breathing Italians. Some allow us to pass when we say 'Permesso' and some don't, and it is clear we might be carried past our destination. For a time I find myself next to a woman less than a metre tall. Looking down at her I say, 'Buon giorno,' at which she giggles into a dirty fur necklet.

Later we visit the British Empire Military Cemetery. I have with me a pot-plant to put on the grave of a friend who lived a few doors from us, and duly see his name on one of the row upon row of white crosses. He is one of 200 Kiwis buried there, and standing by his grave I feel sad once more at the waste of lives.

A Muslim plot nearby consists of large mounds of earth which look desolate. At least the neat white crosses seem more acceptable.

We girls have been granted English leave and Dorraine and I will travel together. Jock's parents are expecting me to visit them in Yorkshire and, while they sound kind, I am filled with dread at the prospect. Full of concern, I feel the urge to explain to them that I did not persuade Jock to break his engagement to the girl they obviously know. I don't want to appear in a bad light, which is vanity I suppose. For my own sake and for Jock's, I am desperately anxious that they should like me.

In preparation for the trip I am buying up tins of fruit and meat for these people who have suffered severe rationing for so long. Although my bag will drag my arms from my body, my popularity should be partly assured.

36

*T*ONE'S GONE. JUST like that. I knew which ship he was going home on and watched the days on my calendar race by as its departure date grew closer. But at the last moment he was transferred to another ship and rushed south without being able to say goodbye.

In the mail I have a brief note from him, and a book I'd lent him, and a comb I'd used for a bookmark. 'I'll write from aboard ship,' is virtually all he says.

I'm pleased neither of us knew our parting was to be this way, and I smile to recall our last time together. Imagine! We were at a party for men going to Japan, and somehow Tone had a staff car. As we were leaving Tone said, 'I've forgotten something,' and dashed back inside the building, returning with an airscrew.

'For you, a present.'

'Not exactly what I most need,' I laughed. 'And how can I take that home to Gisborne?'

The only way the car would accommodate the airscrew was by placing it horizontally out through both open back windows. Tone was extremely pleased when this was finally accomplished, then through the streets of the city we drove like a huge black bird. Avoiding other traffic and lamp-posts presented a minor problem but with some swerving here and there and claiming the middle of the road as ours, we arrived at the Minerva without hurting anyone or anything. It was after midnight. Through the glass revolving door we could see the woggle-woggle man sitting at his desk. When he saw us take the airscrew from the car he left his post and stood perfectly still in the foyer, a mass of glowering disapproval.

Quickly we discovered that it was difficult to worm an airscrew through a revolving doorway. With it balanced at an odd angle, we crouched beside it, trying to be serious for the benefit of the woggle-woggle man, but over and over again when we were ready to step into the foyer, the door returned us to the footpath. The woggle-woggle man was not amused, drawing himself up to his full height and width and waggling his chins.

It took some time for all three of us, Tony, the airscrew and I, to emerge from the door. Politely Tone asked the woggle-woggle man if he would help carry the airscrew to Miss Morrison's room. With a mixture of shock and disdain, the woggle-woggle man lifted one end of the airscrew as Tone lifted the other. Our little entourage took off, painfully negotiating steps, narrow passages and acute corners. Tone was enjoying himself but the woggle-woggle man wasn't, perhaps recognising that his immense size was part of the problem.

On the slender flight of steps leading to my room all became temporarily wedged and had to retreat, but at last the airscrew leant against a wall inside my door. With immobile expressions, Tone and I then followed the woggle-woggle man downstairs, where Tone insisted on shouting him a drink for his kindness. Watching him sip a wine, I knew two things for certain, that he had never heard of the word graciousness, and that it was impossible that I could ever redeem myself in his eyes.

So I have a happy memory of when I last saw Tone and will never be able to recall any painful last-moment goodbyes, where neither knows what to say to the other because words will not convey the real meaning of what is felt.

With Geoff I shared the final goodbye with his parents at Wellington Railway Station and the train took for ever to depart as Geoff and other handsome young airmen sat in their carriages looking out at us as if we were the ones in a cage. The mother of the friend Geoff sat with could not control her tears, and as her son grew white with concern I wished the train would go, although its going would also take Geoff away. I was proud when Geoff took a cigarette from a packet, lit it and put it in his friend's mouth. He was very white himself.

That's what wartime goodbyes are like if you are honest. They are not the happy-go-lucky smiling affairs they might seem to some. They are full of misery, and they are anaemic, and they are horrific, and you never forget them.

As we drove from the station Geoff's father had said, 'He's a good boy.'

'Always has been,' said Sue.

Sitting in the back seat, I said nothing because at that moment there was no place for me in their thoughts. I might not have existed.

So, in a way, I'm glad Tone went without that, without the aches and the tears. Now I'm left to survive, and no one but Tone and I will ever know how we felt about each other. That's the worst thing, really. I'd like to shout it from the rooftops, but you don't do that if you fall in love with a married man. Because falling in love with a married man is wicked and sinful and not to be condoned, although how you stop yourself has never been explained as far as I know. At least I didn't sleep with a married man, much as I'd yearned to. I didn't sleep with the man I loved because he was married to what in songs is called 'another', someone who is probably lovely and beautiful and a superb cook into the bargain. If I ever meet her I'll almost certainly like her, although I won't want to.

It occurred to me before I met Tone that I had never told Jock I loved him. I put 'love' at the end of my letters as I did to everyone, but never did I utter those three beautiful words, 'I love you'. Only Geoff and Tone have heard them from me, Geoff seven years ago for the first time. What I felt for Jock was respect, appreciation, admiration, a multitude of things close to love but not it. In a way I feel guilty for agreeing to become engaged to him, except that at the time I was convinced no one like Geoff would ever enter my life again, and of all the men I had met since his death, Jock came out tops. I thought that was how it was always going to be, the most I could hope for. And I felt very safe with him, which was important and probably selfish. If I judge myself harshly now, it helps to remember that my saying yes brought him happiness for the brief time left to him.

I don't know how I'll fare when things are added up or subtracted, but if you're listening, God, when I said yes to Jock I felt it was right, just as I felt with Tone that being loyal to his wife was right. Now I think both decisions might have been the biggest mistakes I've made in my life. Right or wrong, as sure as hell I'm confused.

I had never thought Tone would write a poem, although he appreciated Byron and Shelley and other thinkers in verse, but from the ship he sends what he says must be the last words he is able to write to me, a poem about poplar leaves dancing their way to earth as we watched them, entranced, on the bank of our stream.

> *To eyes that gazed with such delight*
> *On nature's ways there came sweet peace*
> *Of depth divine to youthful life*
> *Who loves, the reason why not understood.*
> *This wondrous time, when love was found*
> *To be so sweet and warm will live*
> *While other memories fade into the night,*
> *Till life itself takes flight.*

Goodbye, Tone, my love. Goodbye. And thank you.

37

MILAN MUST HOLD a jinx of some sort. We are supposed to be there within eight hours but it takes 17. Although bridge after bridge over the River Po is down there are no notices announcing this until we reach the riverbank and read 'Deviation — Bridge Down', and then we don't need to be told. There is no bridge there.

On our sixth attempt we manage to cross at Casale. Overall we drive many hundreds of extra miles on appalling roads. Every time we are thwarted a sign says 'Milan, 130 kilometres'. Always 130 kilometres. We conclude the notices had been a bulk order. Our maximum speed is 15 kilometres an hour and we crawl into Milan at 4.45 a.m. Understandably our transport officer is not there to meet us but in his bed, so we book in at the Excelsior Officers' Transit Hotel and sleep. Dorraine and I are on our way to England.

We leave Milan tomorrow or the following day and must watch the posting board in the hotel foyer, which is seething with English service folk. The females seem weighed down with rank and call one another 'Miss' or 'Ma'am'. I'd fall over if anyone at our Headquarters called me Miss or Ma'am, and I'd probably laugh. We do not tell a soul that the pips on Dorraine's shoulders are fictitious, that she is, in fact, very non-commissioned. So here we are, two New Zealand WAAC officers complete with pips up, and with black diamonds sewn on our berets. We are unmistakably Kiwis.

Eating breakfast with a group of British nursing sisters who take their rank deeply seriously, I am almost hysterical thinking that if Dorraine were Nan she might say 'Look, you lot, I'm only a corporal and I don't feel the least bit inferior!'

Another look at the notice board tells us that we are to depart at 5.30 p.m. tomorrow, so to fill in time next day we take a tram from the central station into the city where we marvel at the beautiful cathedral with its thousand statues. However, it is so dark inside we can barely see each other, let alone anything else. The scaffolding on which Mussolini and his mistress were hanged still frightens;

the cathedral wall behind it is full of bullet-scars, reminders of Il Duce's supposedly loyal subjects' revenge on his dead body.

We hurry back to the central station, which is colossal and magnificent — and tremendously draughty. Long queues of people lie asleep waiting for booking offices to open. We don't know why they don't all die of pneumonia.

Back at the Officers' Transit Hotel we pack, have a huge bath each and go downstairs for tea. There we meet the British officer (Ma'am) who will be in charge of our rail party to Calais.

Unlike the upholstered seats in the carriage next to us, ours are not, and the four British nursing sisters in our compartment seem close to collapse as a consequence. Their whining worsens as darkness falls and we learn that for some mysterious reason ours is the only carriage to suffer an electrical fault, which means we will travel through the night in total darkness. This adds insult to injury in the eyes of the British nursing sisters. At the first stop, however, a little Italian crawls beneath the carriage and does something magical, and lo, we have lights. Not that this is the end of the complaints. The seats are disgustingly uncomfortable, aren't they, darling, and glory be to God, why don't they do something about the heating? Dorraine and I wonder, too, as like icicles we pass through the Swiss Alps and then gather speed to pass through the Simplon tunnel. A man with limited English explains that the lack of lighting and heating is because this is the only French carriage on the train. Do the French hate us as much as this?

We all warm ourselves a little over cups of tea in the NAAFI carriage in Switzerland, in which neutral country we are forbidden to put a foot on the ground when the train stops. North of the border in France we remain in the NAAFI carriage as long as possible over a lovely meal before returning to our freezing chamber.

Trying to sleep is a problem. Our baggage has been stored away in a special compartment, and Dorraine looks at an empty luggage rack and says 'I'm sleeping up there.' From their expressions, it is clear that the nursing sisters are thinking, 'What can you expect from a girl from the colonies?'

In the morning Dorraine smiles at us all and says, 'I had a beautiful sleep.'

One of the English girls says, 'Really!', in a scathing tone.

'That was a lie, wasn't it?' I whisper to Dorraine later. 'You didn't have a beautiful sleep at all, did you?'

She whispers in return, 'I'm as stiff as a tabletop.'

Other than in Switzerland, at each stop latrines and hot water wait for us, very very welcome. Then we tumble back into our carriage to eavesdrop on the latest scandal about 'Randolph, Churchill's appalling son in ward two my dear, and his Italian girlfriend', and catch up on the news of Skin Jones and Bladder Thompson and Pancreas Sullivan.

Daylight brings views of France which do not stir the senses except for some autumn tints and lacy poplars but at least we are getting closer to the English Channel. At 7 a.m. we reach Calais. We have been on the train for 38 hours.

Leaving the stench of our carriage we climb into a three-ton truck to be driven to the female section of the transit camp, where we eat a memorable meal of chips and real bacon. Our beds are in a huge Nissen hut, and Dorraine and I walk swiftly towards two which are close to a pot-bellied stove and claim them as our own.

We are alarmed as the glances of some present linger on Dorraine. Has word got out that she is not a bona fide officer, or does our guilt misconstrue the reason behind the glances. It could be that the English nursing sisters have spread the news that Dorraine is a mentally unstable Kiwi who sleeps in luggage racks. We wink at each other. We will behave with decorum and innocence, the winks say.

With a few hours to spare we find a Kiwi truck near the camp gate and travel into the city, which is sadly wrecked and almost dead. A few lovely shops are open, their wares expensive beyond belief. Our Italian money has been changed into francs and now we change francs into sterling. After using only paper money for so long, it seems odd having rattling coins again.

At 3.30 p.m., complete with suitcases, we are dropped by truck at the wharf, but by the wrong ship. Is this the French again? we wonder.

As we struggle with our cases to the right ship I know I will arrive on the other side of the Channel with no arms, and I am half wishing I had not bought so many tins of food. On board we join 1500 others, amongst them more than a hundred Kiwi soldiers — men who have travelled from Florence by road. The excitement is intense and becomes more so when less than two hours later we find ourselves standing on deck in sight of land. Although I have never been to England, in my being I feel a surge of pride and belonging as we draw closer and closer to the White Cliffs of Dover.

38

CHAPTER

*A*LL BUT THE Kiwis on board ship leave Folkestone before us, as they have trains to catch. Then we are taken to the Metropole Hotel, where our documentation and pay are organised. I draw £50 plus a little more than three pounds subsistence allowance, and feel very wealthy.

Everslea House, our transit hotel, was once a school. It is typically English, brick, partly three and partly four-storeyed, with wings reaching out left and right from the main central section — a colossal bird emerging from a nest and about to fly away. It is steeply roofed with grey slate and ivy climbs the walls. Between the building and the gate is an expansive lawn dotted with huge old trees, splendid in their mid-winter bareness. In my room I stand at the window smiling, absorbing England.

An inspection of the building takes us up and down steps and stairways, past several interspersed bathrooms and an amusing group of eight wind-blown toilets. None of the light fittings in the bathrooms and toilets have bulbs in them. I discover this when I have a bath before going to bed, and find it necessary to leave the door slightly open so light from the hallway can slip through and I can see the soap. To deter marauding males, I wind one end of my tie around the doorknob and the other end around the useless light switch.

In the morning I am awakened by birdsong and hurry to the window. The sun shines weakly, the grass is green, the unclad trees make magnificent patterns against the sky, and two khaki-clad men stand talking on the lawn, one of them wearing his greatcoat.

When the sergeant-major who manages Everslea House offers me black-market petrol coupons at less than two shillings each I buy 20, reasoning that these can be given to the Schofields to eke out their supplies and at the same time make me more welcome than I might otherwise be.

At our New Zealand Fernleaf Club we lunch with a large group of New

Zealanders before I hail a taxi for the railway station. We have been told we must not give tips to taxi drivers but when I read the meter which says three and threepence I give the driver four shillings, thinking I am being generous. He gives me such a look and says, 'Just the bare fare?' He lifts my suitcase from the car and asks what I have in it — gold bricks. I say, 'Of course, what else?'

I am on my way to see Jock's parents. A soldier sits next to me on the train, and he never stops speaking. Speaking might have been what he was born for. I am becoming quieter and quieter.

Mr Schofield is waiting on the platform. I recognise him instantly, an older version of Jock. He is dressed in a very good quality overcoat, camel-hair I think. He is tall and slim, his back is very straight and he wears glasses. He walks briskly towards me.

As we drive to the house it is clear that our meeting is no easier for him than it is for me, yet like Jock he is kind and thoughtful, doing his best to smooth the way between us, two strangers. He touches my hand as he tells me his wife was too upset to come with him to the station, but adds that I mustn't let myself think she didn't want to.

We park outside a substantial three-storeyed terrace house and Mr Schofield carries my heavy case through the gateway. Before he can put his key in the lock, the door opens and Mrs Schofield, a gentle, sad-looking woman folds me in her arms and cries. A dog runs from somewhere, a cocker-spaniel, and it jumps and jumps up at me, barking joyously. I swear it is smiling.

At this Mrs Schofield, too, smiles briefly. 'He hasn't welcomed anyone like that since Jock was killed,' she says.

'Jock's dog, Glen,' says her husband.

When I present Mrs Schofield with my tinned food, again she overflows with tears, and I feel she always will. And when I give Mr Schofield my black-market petrol coupons, it seems I have placed the sun in his hands.

We are to have a breakfast of bacon and eggs and as I watch Mrs Schofield cutting the rind off the bacon with great concentration, determined not to waste a speck of fat, I think, 'You are unlike me. You are not a survivor,' and I know I will hug her the moment she puts the scissors down.

Soon I am taken upstairs to my bedroom. Jock's bedroom.

'You can put your beret in here,' Mrs Schofield says, opening a drawer. Inside it is Jock's tam-o-shanter with the pom-pom on the top. Hanging in the wardrobe is the kilt I know so well, and beneath the window is his tin trunk with stark white lettering on it — '299284 Lieut J.M. Schofield, Queens Own Cameron Highlanders'.

I lie in Jock's bed but I don't sleep, and at daylight I look across the room at the tin trunk beneath the window. It could be a coffin.

Next day I drive with Mr Schofield to Jock's old school where a memorial service is held for him and two other ex-students who have been killed in action. Mrs Schofield can not face being here. Mr Schofield explains that Jock was to return to be manager of a woollen mill. He says that I will meet Betty, Jock's sister, but that his brother, Ken, is in hospital in London with his broken back.

He takes my hand in his and says the padre found a will in Jock's pocket after he was killed and that I am to have a third of his small estate, Betty and Ken sharing the rest. I weep and say I want to explain to him and to Mrs Schofield that I did not want Jock to break his engagement to the girl they know, that I was brought up not to break up engagements or marriages, and that this has worried me.

'Jock made up his mind, Neva, and you're not to blame yourself for anything. These things have always happened and they always will. And Jock wrote so often of you with such affection. You made him very happy, you must always remember that.'

I want to know how Jock's fiancee responded to her engagement being broken, want to know who she is. I wonder at the memorial service, is she here? Is the young woman who has perhaps loved Jock in the way I have loved Geoff and Tone, in this hall? Is she looking at me sitting with Jock's father, resenting me? But I will never know the answer to any of these things. She is never mentioned.

As the train pulls out of the station taking me back to London I wish I had given more to Jock, but I gave all I could. I'd have been dishonest had I given more.

A religious woman sits alongside me in the train. Her son is in heaven, she confides. And when we part, she says 'Goodbye, dear. We'll meet again,' and she looks at the sky.

39
CHAPTER

*D*ORRAINE AND I travel back to Florence via Genoa, with its lovely architecture and harbour, its palms and gardens and fountains; then down to Spezia where Shelley was drowned when his yacht was wrecked, and Pisa, where we climb the Leaning Tower and swing on the bells with a great sense of power.

All but one girl gives us a warm welcome back and are agog to hear what lies ahead for them on their own English leave. But my foot is barely in the office door when the girl who deputised for me while I was away walks in scowling. At length she complains that she had had no idea how busy she would be in my absence and in an aggrieved voice implies that I should not have taken leave. She has never forgiven me for being commissioned ahead of her.

At a personal level I am very difficult to make angry, but I am angry now. As I simmer I remember Tone again, hear his advice inside my head, remember Jock's parents, too, and the sadness that has visited their home. And I think of my own grieving.

I tell the girl it was the brigadier who decided that as officer commanding the WAACs I should be one of the first girls to take English leave. I tell her that it is unnecessary, unkind, unjust and unacceptable that she should attack me in this way. I tell her it is unworthy of her. And I remind her that we are serving in a war, for God's sake, and that her complaint of overwork is so trivial it is laughable. I speak softly, believing that there is immense power in quiet wrath.

Smiling, I promise that after doing her job as well as mine while she is on her own English leave, I will not batter her with a tirade as she has me. And I ask her to remember that I am her commanding officer, something I have not said to anyone before and hope I will never feel it necessary to say again. Then I tell her to go away.

At breakfast next morning she is so charming I understand how easy it would be to commit murder.

Things are fairly chaotic. Hundreds of men are going home, which means a lot of documentation. Eight girls from down south are joining us, there is a farewell to the principal matron, and five of our original girls are packing up to depart on the *Orion*, one of four troopships arriving within a fortnight of one another. Their capacity is 13,000, and 1400 of the men listed to go home on them are on English leave, so the brigadier is urging that the sailing of the *Orion* be deferred for two weeks. Some men who have already sailed have resented the presence on board of Italian wives and fiancees who have been allotted comfortable cabins.

Injections continue. Until the very last girl departs these must be kept current, and right now we have a few wrecks as always after what we call jabbing day.

Something that happens is a little eerie. A corporal from the Legal Section takes me to a ballet at the Verdi Theatre, which is packed with Italians. We are the only Allied personnel in the audience. There are often cries of 'Down with the Americans', and 'Down with the English' and 'Up with the Italians'. Each time this happens countless eyes stare at us to see how we are reacting. We appear to be in deep conversation with each other, as if unaware of the insults.

BROWNIE AND BILL have looked at several locations while on their honeymoon, deciding where they might settle and open a business of their own, as Bill is determined, after being a prisoner of war for so long, that he will be his own boss and not return to being a stock agent. Brownie writes:

4 October 1945.
Bill has fallen in love with Russell and wants to buy a place and live here. It's miles away from anywhere, and when you do reach the end of the road, you travel by launch to get here.

It's the most primitive place, with no sewerage, and the Strand, which is the main road, is just earth. Cattle roam every street. The people are all related and are very conservative and don't want new blood in the village as they prefer the place to remain as it was in 1840. They're afraid a newcomer might build a new house, or a new shop, or try to put the pictures on three times a week instead of once. Someone might even bring a car into Russell, which would upset the cattle.

I send Brownie a statue of 'The Dying Gaul', which cost me thousands of lire, and, to pay for it, I had to borrow cigarettes galore from anyone willing to take me on as a financial risk.

Someone in Signals mends my iron for me. He so appreciates being made to feel useful he sends me a huge bunch of roses, and I am so appreciative of these that he presents me with a folding umbrella in various shades of brown. This brings a flood of gratitude, so now he is making me a crystal set. Where will it end? This man calls me his 'old amico'.

Our lovely Min is being invalided home with anxiety neurosis. Her behaviour is not at all like S's. Other than using sticking plaster as a wrinkle deterrent, she has never done anything noticeably crazy. She has simply become uncharacteristically withdrawn, as if her mind is a spider scuttling to dark corners.

It is hard to find a reason for this as she has been so popular, but whatever the cause, her emotions have obviously turned cartwheels. As far as any of us knows, she hasn't had to contend with any insurmountable problems, and it seems that her great attributes of beauty and popularity might have been her downfall. They are a large credit on one side of her personal ledger, but somehow her emotional books don't balance. She is out of sync.

40
CHAPTER

ON MY CRYSTAL set I listen to the life story of John McCormack, the Irish singer, who has just died. He made his debut at Covent Gardens in 1907 at the age of 14 in *Cavalleria Rusticana* of all things. In my memory I can hear the recordings of his we used to play on our wind-up gramophone at home, though they were not opera. What I hear are old familiar Irish tunes like 'The Mountains of Mourne' and 'A Dear Little Town in the old County Down', songs to make my father smile as he is reminded of his homeland. I remember, too, 'The Whistler and His Dog', and 'If I had the Wings of an Angel' and 'Watchman, What o' the Night', and the voices of Galla Curci and Enrico Caruso. Then there was the first copy of 'Pokarekare Ana' with the lovely voices of Ana Hato and her cousin, Dean Waratene. I can still feel the gradual stiffening of the handle as we wind the machine up. And I can see the short sharp His Master's Voice gramophone needles in a minute tin with a hinged lid and a blue label — *be careful now, don't spill them.*

Along with 50 others, I go to a Jayforce 25th Battery farewell party at the Excelsior Hotel by the Ponte Santa Trinita, which spans the Arno. We dine at a single long table and afterwards do the Palais Glide, and dance and sing 'The Lambeth Walk'.

> *Any time you're Lambeth way,*
> *Any evening, any day,*
> *You'll find us all*
> *Doing the Lambeth Walk.*

On Christmas morning I open a small parcel wrapped in green tissue paper and gasp. In my hand I hold the Hebe and Eagle cameo I so admired as the carver worked on it when I visited the factory with 'my amico'. The carver explained that Jupiter fell in love with Hebe, who unfortunately loved only birds, so Jupiter wisely had himself turned into an eagle. My cameo depicts Hebe feeding Jupiter from a bowl on her knee. A note comes with the gift, 'To my old amico. May faith and joy be yours in full measure.' Faith and joy, two lovely words I've no trust in, but a beautiful wish.

With Jayforce folk departing and others going home, there are several parties at Headquarters, and a lot of exhausted people. At one party it is announced that the Italian countess present will cut the cake. Our chief matron, who should be asked to cut the cake, watches, pretending not to hear a loud Kiwi voice say, 'Damned rude and in poor taste. The countess might be a countess but she's still only an Eyetie bint.'

Next morning one of our colonels phones me to ask if I know which of my girls put on his head the little red Tyrolean hat he found himself wearing when he reached his mess last night.

In our office chaos continues. Signals and ciphers are coming and going and sheets of paper flurry like autumn leaves. Every movement of every soldier must be documented by every department of 2 NZEF, and with so many things happening simultaneously, the world of words is going mad. An air of frantic urgency envelops headquarters as typists belt away with carbon and foolscap and quarto and octavo paper, and officers' fingers ache as they sign their names over and over and over again.

'When are you going home, Neva?' someone asks.

'I'm staying behind for as long as I can.'

'Don't you want to go home?'

'Oh, God, yes.'

'Well?'

'If you pull my fingernails out, I'm still not going to tell you,' I say.

41
CHAPTER

W E PREPARE TO leave the Minerva Hotel. I oversee tin trunks being loaded on to trucks which are about to take off when a girl rushes up to me, followed by the furious and voluble hotel owner. She has told him that she has mistakenly packed a sheet belonging to him. I wish she had had the sense not to mention the sheet. In the overall picture, it seems singularly unimportant and now we have a private war on our hands.

The Italian waves his arms at me and I nod that I understand, and promise that the moment the tin trunk concerned reaches Bari the sheet will be returned to him. To assure him that I mean what I say, I take my little notebook from my battle-dress pocket and scribble a message to myself, 'Return sheet to grizzlepuss at Minerva.'

Some of us have dealt with the trunks of girls still on English leave, and somehow one gets left behind in a bedroom. There is an insane dash upstairs at the last moment to get it. And as the truck driver revs up his motor and takes off, a girl asks where she can get sanitary towels.

I point to the back of the truck. 'There,' I say. The truck is turning a corner. Then it is out of sight.

Brigadier Stevens took over some time ago from General Freyberg, so instead of being OICA, Officer in Charge of Administration, he is GOC, General Officer Commanding.

He informs me that, until we move south to Bari where the Rear Party will be stationed, Nan and I will stay at the beautiful Excelsior Hotel along with himself and a handful of others. We go there right away. Our room, number 240, is spacious, and our ensuite bathroom is luxurious beyond comprehension. From a wall Madame le Brun's self-portrait looks down on us. On our balcony two Union Jacks fly.

General Stevens takes me on a last tour of Firenze. We visit the chapel at

Palazzo Medici to view the frescoes before carrying on to the Chapel of Prince Lorenzo where the angle of the stone defines the colours of the marble inlays. Here we see the crests of every Tuscan town of any size, San Gimignano of tower fame, Assisi, Pisa, et cetera, and that of Firenze of course, with its famous Florentine lily.

On leaving for the south I travel with the general in his staff car. Mid-afternoon we arrive at Rome's Eden Hotel, which is reserved for senior officers and their wives. Each time the staff addresses me as Mrs Stevens, the general and I smile for a reason they don't understand.

In the morning we drive down Route 7 for some distance, but it is so dangerously covered with snow that we return and take Route 6 through the arable acres of the Pontine Marshes, drained by Mussolini.

At Bari our offices are warmer than the mess, which is part of a hospital. One of our girls has been interviewed for work with the United Nations Rest and Rehabilitation Administration (UNRRA) instead of going home, and Nan and I are on the list to go to Japan.

With us here are Italian wives and fiancees of some of our men, German prisoners of war who are painting our numbers and names and addresses on our tin trunks, and seven Chinese. Where the Chinese have come from and where they are going I have yet to discover. It looks as if God has reached down with a colossal hand, picked up a cluster of human beings, shaken them about like dice, and dropped us all on this spot.

The matron of the hospital quarters of which we are part shows every sign of disliking us. She calls me to her office to complain that I have not put in any personnel returns since our arrival, which is nonsense; each day I have handed one to the duty officer. Because we swell the numbers I am strangely responsible for getting extra charcoal to heat the irons, and must also find a shoemaker when shoemakers seem non-existent. It will be a relief when the *Tamaroa* pulls out and leaves only our Rear Party.

IT IS SEVEN years ago today since Geoff and I decided we would be married. We were sitting in his car, Theodora, on the top of Gray's Hill, looking down over the Poverty Bay flats and across the water to Young Nicks Head and the world, and the years yawning ahead were ours, or so we thought. We did not doubt that we could spread out a blanket of life and tuck in the edges. Smiling, I think of us sitting there, two pleasant people. Without him now, and without Tone, there are no edges to tuck in. The war has stolen all certainties from us, wherever we are and whoever we are. Everyone.

I think of Tone. He will never replace Geoff in my memory of course. No one ever will, and I think Tone would be comfortable with that. I doubt, though, that Geoff would understand my loving another man. But I do, and Tone is alive and I want to be close to him, to hear his voice and his laugh, want to feel the magic of his touch. He lit a lamp in my being, although he was not entirely mine, nor ever will be. Bits of him, the biggest bits, will always be somewhere else, with someone else.

For me there are fragments of consolation I'll carry around with me always, and if at times I might cry, I will laugh too. Howard the Scot need not worry. I won't forget what he said, 'Keep your sense of humour or you'll be sunk.' Wherever I go I'll carry a baggage of the ludicrous with me, because that's what we are, perhaps, all slightly ridiculous and unimportant. I thought that as I sat on top of Casteletto Inferiore in the Dolomites, and I think it now. Yet how can I say that? How can I say individuals are unimportant and at the same time carry fragments of them with me always? You see, I am confused. I don't know where my thoughts are taking me and I'm incapable of clarifying them right now.

If I am less pleasant than I once was, and I know I am, I have learned something of the new me. I understand the reasons for the anger inside me, and I have learned, too, to place a value on my own opinions, realising that they might be as valid as those of anyone else, notwithstanding who that is. I have rubbed shoulders with many holding superior ranks who have come from high positions in civilian life and I have had time to evaluate them not as managers of a business or officers in an army but as human beings who might sit at my table. It is strangely comforting to know that they are as strong and as weak as I, a minion in their midst.

None of the girls are aware of how I feel, even Nan. What they see is the Neva they have always known, calm and happy. They know nothing of what is hidden away, too hurtful to speak of and too precious to share.

42

N^AN AND I have walked around Bari and into the hinterland and are appalled at the squalor of Southern Italy, the filth and poverty and the stinking hovels. We are pleased we've had typhoid jabs. We see no smiles from the peasants, just hang-dog looks and drab clothing, but the priests we pass look healthy and happy and well-fed. No filth there, nor any sign of poverty. They smile. Their cheeks are rosy. It all seems grossly unfair.

For some time I watch a German prisoner of war completing the lettering on a tin trunk with his slender paint-brush. In a fine tenor voice, he usually sings as he works. I interrupt him to praise what he is doing and he stands and smiles at me.

'You're not singing today,' I say.

'It is the birthday of my mother and I am unhappy. I hear nothing from my family for a long long time. My home is in the Russian zone, you understand.'

I look at this young man who can print so perfectly and sing like an angel.

'I have a crystal set, a radio. You know what I mean?'

'Ja.'

'When I leave here, I'll give it to you.'

'Funkgerat!' the young man exclaims. In German he says more, none of which I understand.

'You have a lovely voice,' I tell him. 'Will you sing in a concert we are having?'

'Ja, ja, I will sing,' he answers, and he kisses both of my cheeks.

Later I take out my German/English dictionary which instructs me how to ask a soldier if he is Albanian, Czech, Bulgarian or Danish. It tells me how to enquire as to the whereabouts of the railroad and the power plant and the river, and how to say 'Look out' and 'Don't smoke' and 'Obey or I'll fire'. Funkgerat, I discover, simply means radio.

At the concert the general has me sing my silly little pansy face song with my toes turned in, and there is laughter. When the German boy sings 'Holy City' it is so beautiful we all want to cry.

When the girls know I am giving my radio to the German boy my old adversary protests severely that this is wrong.

'He's an enemy,' she says, 'and my brother's a prisoner of war in German hands.'

'And I've had two fiances killed by the enemy,' is all I say. I do not add that to me the German is as fine a young man as any fine young man in the Allied forces, and that almost certainly he had not wanted to kill any more than Geoff or Jock had. Like our men, he is a pawn in a ghastly game being played by political manipulators. His being an enemy is simply a matter of where he was born.

A message arrives from Army Headquarters in New Zealand that approval has been given for Nan and me to go to Japan, but a second message counters it. Mrs Jowett, Chief NZWAAC in Wellington has decreed that there are others who, as she puts it, haven't had the chance to go overseas, so we will be returning home. Does she, like many ordinary New Zealanders, think that we have been over here doing nothing but have a wonderful time, that we've been on a fun junket? Has she seen S. or Min since their return home? Has she the remotest idea of what being on active service as a WAAC is like as she sits in her comfy cushioned office powdering her nose?

General Stevens is an angel of a man. He is arranging for me to fly to Egypt rather than go by ship so I can visit Geoff's grave at Benghazi, and he will have a male officer accompany me. I am overcome. With all his busyness, this exalted man has room in his thinking for someone as unexalted as I.

'I'll be grateful to you until I die,' I tell him.

'Yes, yes,' he replies gruffly, 'that's very nice.' But he smiles.

43
CHAPTER

I AM TO fly to Egypt with General Stevens and my escort officer and I will join
the *Arawa* at Tewfik after visiting Geoff's grave. The girls have been instructed
to leave the airscrew behind when they leave Bari. Transporting it to Gisborne
could be difficult, it would mean explanations to Mum and Dad, and I need no
such blatant reminder of Tone.

Preparing to leave, we pack our trunks. I've acquired a metal ammunition box
which the singing German addresses for me, and I certainly need it to
accommodate the accumulation of purchases I must get home to New Zealand:
two surplus fluffy khaki blankets, surplus cigarettes galore which Brownie and
Bill will enjoy, two bottles of whisky which I loathe, and some excellent library
books.

After an early breakfast I depart for the airport with Captain Morris to find
General Stevens already there. In my hand I clutch a bunch of roses given me by
the girls. Around their stalks is a damp khaki stocking, and a note with them
reads, 'To a grand kid, from all her blokes.' Do other commanding officers receive
such a beautiful messages, I wonder? It is a simple treasure to hold in my mind
always. But when I show it to the captain he says, 'Quite insincere.'

When tickets for Cairo are issued this cynical officer and I are the only two
left waiting. A pilot-officer steps into the plane with the remaining tickets and
when he emerges, we suggest they might be ours. He shakes his head. No, they
are for two brothers. Then General Stevens emerges from the aircraft. It is a mix-
up, he explains brusquely, the officer and I share similar surnames, Morris and
Morrison, and the tickets are definitely ours. The pilot-officer doesn't look
altogether pleased with us for not being brothers.

The plane is an old and decrepit converted parachute Dakota with two rows
of cold bucket seats facing the centre. As we take off I look back at the country
in which I leave a part of my being. Lest I fall apart in what feels like a bucketful

of bolts, I discipline myself to gather the fragments of my Italian experience together like the pieces of a jig-saw puzzle.

Crossing the Mediterranean is uneventful until we almost reach land and the plane begins to sound different. It will be because the pilot is descending, my escort says.

'Are you sure?'

'Haven't you flown before?' he asks.

'In a tiny plane that behaved itself much better than this model.'

I am told I am being fussy.

When we land at Bernini in the middle of the desert and the pilot reveals that one engine had been giving trouble I jab my companion in the ribs, but he pretends not to notice.

He and I have to find our own transport to Benghazi (or Bengasi, as it is spelt here). As he is going on to Cairo when the aircraft's ailment is remedied, the general says he will see us on the Wellington wharf when the *Arawa* berths, that we are to look for him waving a small Union Jack.

In a Royal Signals jeep the captain and I travel to Benghazi, where a handful of Jews live, although the Italian origin of most of the inhabitants is reflected in the trees and houses of the town whose softness and shade must have been a haven to soldiers after serving in the desert 18 kilometres away.

We find our way to the office of the Town Major/Camp Commandant where we are sent upstairs to the Graves Registration Unit. There the officer in charge drops what he is doing and drives us to another office where registers are kept. Geoff's death is not listed. This shocks me. I explain that two years ago the Imperial War Graves Commission wrote that this is where Geoff is buried.

'Yes,' replies the officer, 'but no record is kept of unidentifiable bodies and you say your fiancé was one of three in his aircraft who couldn't be identified.'

'That's right, but why aren't such men recorded?'

'Because a mistake might occur. Somehow a chap might get out of it and if he'd been recorded as being killed it would complicate things.'

I can see that. The books have to be kept straight, and recording the burials of human remains, identifiable or not, can be equated with journal entries in a book-keeping system. Skeletal items must be accurately accountable, so when the auditor comes along there is no confusion.

Now I am in the situation of an auditor and I desperately want to know where exactly Geoff is buried.

We are taken to the cemetery and left there for a time. The War Graves Commission had informed me that a memorial was to be erected here with the names of unidentifiable personnel on it, but there is no evidence of it yet, no sign whatever of 41308 Pilot-Officer Geoffrey Pender Chambers.

Captain Morris and I walk past row upon row of white crosses. Twelve graves are marked, 'Unknown-RAF' and three are marked, 'Three unknown RAF'.

I put the flowers the girls have given me on the first of the graves marked 'Three unknown RAF' and stand back, imagining how fierce the heat must have been to have totally destroyed Geoff's asbestos identity disc as he was shot down in flames, the one terrible fear he had. In silence the captain stands beside me.

'It might not even be his grave,' I say, and I cry and cry. I want so much to talk to Geoff and I can't because I don't know if he is where I have put the flowers. I will have to pretend, which I don't like, because the love we had shared had nothing to do with pretending. It was real and for always. No one would ever replace what we had known even if it is possible to love someone else in a different way. I want to tell him this, to tell him that in my heart the pain will always be immeasurable. But how can I tell this to someone whose remains might not be his?

I almost do not notice that Captain Morris puts a lighted cigarette in my non-smoking mouth and when I do realise it is there I move away, smoking it, to the other two graves of the 'Three unknown RAF', wondering, if this is where the flowers should be. And I will never know. I will never know exactly where the bones of the one great love of my life lie and I know I will always be consumed by not knowing.

The captain is by my side now, with a hand on my shoulder.

'I want to know,' I say. 'Which one?'

'You've got to be realistic, Neva. It doesn't matter which.'

He doesn't understand at all, I think. He is thinking with his head and I am thinking with my heart. I walk away, wanting to be alone as I cry because my tears are private to Geoff and myself. I know that if he could, Geoff would be crying too. Somewhere in behind my nose there is an enormous ache.

44
CHAPTER

*O*UR PLANE IS still 'out the monk' as they say. The pilot has cleaned the spark plugs which he thought were offending but is not happy, so has had others flown from Cairo. Still the aircraft complains. The general and the captain and I have been allocated to another Dakota, which will fly out in the morning. For the night I will share a Nissen hut equipped for 14 with a British junior commander.

Eggs and tomatoes are laid on incessantly in the dining-room, and one pilot tells me he has a solid layer of eggs inside him, which I can understand. I notice that meal sittings are remarkably long, there being nothing else to do. Eating eggs fills in time as it does stomachs.

On our flight we pass Wadi Matruh from which soda is extracted to make soap for Egypt. We see Bardia out on a peninsula and fly over Sellum, and then Tobruk where six ships are anchored. Fort Capuzzo looks like something from *Beau Geste*, and then comes Hellfaya Pass. From our height we can not perceive its steepness. The Nile is a long wriggling worm, and from where we are the pyramids are tiny. Bathed in a soft glow reflected from a vivid Egyptian sunset is Cairo.

At the airport we have a meal while our luggage is searched. Riots in Cairo keep the city out of bounds. An RAF bus is to take us to the Heliopolis Palace Hotel when the riots are over, but waiting does not appeal to General Stevens who strides back and forth impatiently.

'All this business of the riots is being grossly overdone,' he assures Captain Morris and me.

Like the pilot-officer at the airport in Italy, the man behind the hotel desk mistakes the names of the captain and myself and books us into a double room.

Infuriated, General Stevens sits me on the counter. 'Look' he says, 'this is a female and that officer there is a male, and their names are different. They need separate rooms.'

The intimidated clerk organises this, but warns me that I must be careful. The reason for this I find when I use my ensuite bathroom. It is also the ensuite bathroom for a man in a room through another door and at times he and I lock one another out of our shared bathroom, which brings some hilarity to our short stay in the hotel.

In the morning Cairo is still out of bounds and I discover a peculiar thing. When there is to be rioting, the times of opening and closing are advertised in the newspaper.

Maadi Camp has been instructed to send an armoured car to the hotel for us, in which case I am to be rear gunner, but instead a staff car arrives. Into it the general and the captain and I creep, the driver and each passenger equipped with a pistol. Driving quickly through Cairo, we pass several groups of armed men and a number of trucks carrying Egyptian soldiers. We are told to say we are Kiwis and not British if we are stopped, as Kiwis are popular and the British are not, but we don't have that excitement.

The WAAC compound is surrounded by scrub fences, Only six girls remain here. No building is left unlocked because the Egyptians, who steal freely, are familiar with the movements of everyone in the camp and even elude the guards who are on duty from dusk until dawn. I am pleased I have not served here in the sand and wind and sterility, not to mention the Egyptians.

With the general, I attend the unveiling of the Maadi Memorial, a gift to the people of the village from the soldiers who have passed through Maadi Camp. On one side of the obelisk is a high garden in which flowers have yet to be planted. On the other side is a slab of black marble. On the obelisk itself a kiwi, a fernleaf and the Southern Cross are carved, and at the top is a New Zealand 'Onward' badge.

The general makes a speech, thanking the villagers who have worked in the Maadi tent or helped our men in any way. While we are at the unveiling the 'wogs' steal all the primuses in the compound.

While the girls here are at work next day I wash my hair and protect the compound, armed with a revolver I have no idea how to use. As far as I know no thief comes near the place.

For three days Cairo is out of bounds again. The students responsible are said to have the backing of important people, and word has it that any British vehicle or soldier will be attacked on sight. The students are described as being 'educated young men with the interests of their country at heart'.

The strain of doing so little here is wearing. I have played crib until I fall asleep, I've collected my washing from the *dobi* down through the dump and I've written letters by the acre. I've been to the shoemaker's to have plates put on the heels of my shoes and I've read Ann Bridge's *Peking Picnic* and Catherine Cotton's marvellous *Experience*. I've been to the officers' shop with a man who tells me he once took £80,000 to Barclay's Bank through the dodgy Cairo traffic. Even without the stones and bullets, surely this is enough to earn him a war ribbon for 'Action in Cairo'.

The bull ants at Maadi fascinate me. Why do they climb a five-metre wall to get inside the compound, when two centimetres away there is no wall? Are they blind or stupid? It is futile blowing on them when they walk on your skin, as they just hang on and turn into the wind. The only effective thing to do is to hit them with a shoe. This is another thing I have been doing to fill in time and getting paid for it. Hitting ants with a shoe. It is tedious beyond belief.

According to the newspaper, the Cairo riots have been postponed until Tuesday, so Dot and I go into the Mouski where she buys me a beautiful brass Persian tray and I buy her a snakeskin compact which is quite lovely, although I am saddened to think of the sacrifice made by the snake.

We then see Katharine Hepburn and Spencer Tracy in *Without Love* at the Metro Theatre before going to Peanut Alley to buy peanuts to take aboard the *Arawa*. We have a gin and squash at the Manhattan Bar and a Brazilian iced chocolate somewhere else, and eat dinner at the Regent Hotel. Then we taxi back to the camp, singing in what we imagine is harmony.

At last I am leaving here. Thank God.

Up at 4.45 a.m., and at seven o'clock exactly we leave Maadi Camp. We travel in trucks carrying spare 'Tommy' drivers. They will return the trucks to Maadi Camp, which is being taken over by the British. The leading truck breaks down in the Dead City and ours has to push it out, then a second truck breaks down and we tow it for the next 140 kilometres.

Cairo's riot is to begin at 8 a.m. The 'Wog' army is on alert, and more soldiers are streaming into the city, ready for the affray. This is to be Cairo's largest riot and British citizens have been warned that they will be attacked if they appear on the streets. We scrape through the city at exactly 7.50 a.m.

As we tumble out of the truck at Tewfik I see the girls leaning over the rail of the *Arawa* and we act like schoolchildren, calling and waving as if we've been apart for years rather than days. I make my way along the bustling wharf with its black and white faces and its piles of luggage and cartons of food. The voices of the workers are raised in what seems anger as orders are shouted in rapid Arabic. The air is hot.

Climbing the gangway carrying my kitbag with a huge package of peanuts in it, I wave with my free hand from time to time. On deck I want to hug everyone on sight.

A duty officer tells me I am to share a cabin with two nurses and three of my own Clerical Divison girls. Then Nan and another girl accompany me to the cabin. As we enter it, Nan says, 'Surprise, surprise.'

My mouth opens. 'Oh, God!' I say. 'You devils!' Leaning against my bunk is Tone's airscrew.

45
CHAPTER

WITH OTHERS I sit in shorts on deck in the afternoon, not hidden away in a separate area as we were en route from New Zealand. Here we girls are able not only to smile at the men but to speak to them. It seems we are on a cruise ship, and it is clear that army regulations are not going to apply.

Although some of us do any typing necessary, for the most part we can choose what we do with our time. I nurse a private hope that no officer on board is going to have me record his sexual exploits as my Lecherous Major did on the way over.

Ship's concerts are being organised by a Catholic priest from Sydney and before I came aboard the girls volunteered my services to sing.

In the evening we play housey in the lounge and our cabin nets almost four pounds, not a penny of it mine.

The ship's hospital is out of bounds for visitors as it is full of influenza patients. In this hot climate why do people get flu? I thought flu was reserved for winter temperatures.

Two nights out and there is a quiz session with somewhat childish questions such as, 'What did Margaret Mitchell say when her hat blew off?' Answer, 'Gone with the wind.' And there is the gag about day breaking and night falling. We learn that apes differ from monkeys in that they have no tails, and that proportionately speaking, of all creatures the ant has the largest brain. Has no one heard of the bull ants at Maadi, which haven't any?

In a concert a lieutenant wearing no expression delivers a limerick which appeals:

There was a young poet of Japan
Who found that his lines didn't scan.
When asked why it was
He said 'It's because
I try to get as many words into the last line as I possibly can.'

An Australian tenor and I sing 'Memory Lane', 'You'll Never Know' and 'You're Mine'.

We are melting with the heat. Yet still we play tenniquoits, bathed in perspiration.

On our second night at sea we listen to a talk, 'The Atom Bomb. Should Peacetime Armies Be Increased?' The war has just ended and we are asked to think like this? How can there ever be peace?

At 4 p.m. we reach Aden, where there is no organised shore leave, so in a very haphazard way we are taken to the town in every imaginable type of small craft. When we leave early in the morning all hands are present, plus three monkeys, one of which has stolen an officer's favourite pair of socks.

Shadows at midday are nil. It's hard to imagine a world without the beauty they bring, the various shades of grey, hard to think of a world without their softness, as they dapple the landscape, and provide shade for the animals in the fields. But we are crossing the equator and there is not a shadow in sight. The sea is so calm it could be a sheet of the palest blue paper, and last night the sun dipped over the horizon at precisely six o'clock in a blaze of glory which stretched from left to right, as if the huge red orb was embracing as much of the world as it could hold.

We are having tropical storms, which arrive with such suddenness that when on deck we see a square inch of black cloud we hustle for the lounge before a downpour descends upon us. If we get caught our wet bodies steam.

Funny little Chad figures are appearing on the notice-board. Peering over a wall is a head with three spikes of hair. Two sets of fingers grip the wall. Beneath is a phrase, 'Wot no something-or-other.' Today a 'Brains Trust' notice lists the personnel who will take part, all colonels, flight lieutenants, et cetera, and there is Chad saying, 'Wot, no privates!'

WHEN WE APPROACH Fremantle a band plays vigorously as a crowd waits to welcome home the 'Westralians'. Then a group of us go into Perth for a meal at the Esplanade Hotel where lamb and mint sauce have never tasted so good. A lot of sodden types stagger aboard later, and three Kiwis are missing. The number of days it takes our ship to reach New Zealand will be taken off their leave entitlement and they will have to pay their own fares home. After being on active service!

Most of those who can still stand up watch the brilliance of Aurora Australis before going to bed, on a night so deathly still and cloudless no one wants to speak above a whisper.

Sailing into the Australian Bight brings loud choruses of 'The Tattooed Lady':

I paid ten cents to see a fair tattooed lady,
Around her hips was a row of battleships,
And right across her jaw was Australia's sunny shore.
On her chest was an opossum, with its tail, red, white and blue,
And on her back was a Union Jack and a bloody great kangaroo.
The map of Germany was where it ought to be,
And on her kidney, yes, her kidney, was a bird's-eye view of Sydney.
Around the corner, the Johnny Horner, was my home in . . .

The last words are drowned out, a mixture of 'Bondi Beach', 'Saint Kilda', 'Wellington', 'Auckland', et cetera.

We have our last concert, and the Catholic padre asks us all to a party in his cabin afterwards. We decide to arrive carrying the airscrew and present it to him, so we autograph it, then sit a bottle of gin in the hole before setting off. As we struggle through the padre's doorway he is speechless. With delight, he says.

When we berth at Melbourne the pilot brings New Zealand mail aboard. Brownie says she and Bill will be in Wellington to meet the *Arawa*, Dad says he supposes I've learned a lot while I've been away, and Mum says the cat has eaten the canary.

By the time all the Australians have disembarked the city's shops are closed, but some of us go ashore. The most exciting thing a group of us do is have a double-malted milk-shake. Then we walk on the bank of the Yarra and taxi back to the ship.

Cables from friends are arriving and we are being issued with our free rail warrants and ration coupons. The atmosphere is very subdued as a lot of civilians have come aboard in place of the Australian troops and we feel obliged to behave as quietly as they do, which is quite a strain as we cross the Tasman.

I do not share the excitement of others on board as we approach New Zealand but try to conceal this as I join others lining the deck rail where we scan the horizon for the first sighting of the coastline. After a long time someone shouts and points, 'There!' We all rush to give tips to cabin, bath and mess stewards before returning to the deck to say goodbye to our friends.

We line the rail again as our homeland looms closer. Although I have so dreaded returning, and hold a solid stone of fear in my heart, a huge well of pride in my country surges through me.

THE MAGIC OF Wellington Harbour on such a still fine day as this! Eastbourne and Day's Bay hug the shoreline on our right and Island Bay lazes in the sun on the left as we pass Barretts Reef. Before long the heights of Roseneath are full of eyes looking down on us. Then the city spreads itself before us with its office blocks and harbour buildings and wharves. Mount Victoria, with its myriad of little boxes clinging to it as if by magic. smiles in the sun. Sitting in the shade across the water, larger homes on other hilltop suburbs thumb their noses at their poor relations. Now I can see Sue's apartment, the window from which she waved a tea-towel as we left the harbour so long ago.

We are all very quiet as the *Arawa* slowly approaches the wharf.

Suddenly I wave. There is Sue. And Brownie and Bill are waving two hands each, Bill tall and handsome and very thin. The staff of Sick and Wounded are there, too, as they were when I left New Zealand. An officer from the Gisborne Army Office stands by the foot of the gangway, and alongside him, holding a small Union Jack high in the air, is General Stevens.

Together Nan and I disembark. When I reach the general he lifts me in the air with excitement and says, 'I told you I'd be here.' Brownie and Bill say I look different and I say so do they; Sue kisses and hugs me and hands me a box of chocolates; a man from Sick and Wounded gives me a bunch of carnations and the biggest hug in the world; the Gisborne officer brings messages from the drill hall staff and kisses me with his nail-brush moustache; and before we can think we are being hustled towards a bus marked 'Hawke's Bay and Gisborne'.

At every stop the bus makes to let returning men off someone is waiting to say hello — at Levin and Dannevirke and Palmerston North and Hastings, and at Napier where Nan leaves the bus. We two part sadly, but keep smiling.

There are still about 215 kilometres to go and apart from the driver and myself there is only one soldier carrying on to Gisborne. This man leaves his seat at the back of the bus and sits next to me. He is short, with ridiculously broad shoulders, no neck to speak of and a pugnacious face. I recognise him as belonging to a family of brothers who were in gaol more often than not. For a crime of some sort committed in Egypt, this one has peeled potatoes all the way home on the *Arawa*.

Our conversation is not scintillating but it fills in time, and although I hope he will fall asleep he shows no sign of it whatever. On we talk.

We descend from the Whareratas on to the flats and are passing Young Nicks Head before circling the inner reaches of Poverty Bay when the soldier says, 'You and me get on together good. I'll phone youse one of these days.'

At almost 2 a.m. we reach the Gisborne Drill Hall. Waiting outside to meet me are Mum and Dad, an aunt and Howard the Scot.

We all put our arms around one another and weep a little. All but Howard, that is. Setting himself up in charge of us, he soon puts a stop to that. A Red Cross car has been organised to take us all home, he says, and he hopes I remembered what he had told me, to keep my sense of humour.

'Every time I almost lost it, I thought of you,' I say.

In the Red Cross car I can feel Mum and Dad and my aunt smiling in the dark, and I am smiling too. I am home whether I like it or not.

46
CHAPTER

A LETTER ARRIVES from Wellington, asking me to join the Public Service, and I quail, recalling how little respect I've ever had for government departments, how I have always thought them over-staffed and dull. I write saying that only a position that is stimulating in a stimulating department would appeal, otherwise I am not interested. I am amazed at my audacity as I wait for a reply.

I go to a party where a doctor plays music on a saw and his wife looks cunningly at me and supposes I have a lover or two.

'One or two!' I say, and want to go home.

A neighbour comes to visit and tells me how terrible it has been with all the rationing. 'You've no idea, Neva,' she says, shaking her head.

'It must have been dreadful,' I say.

A friend of my parents says she supposes I'll marry and settle down with one of the locals now that I've had that wonderful experience and I say 'Perhaps'.

Another says, 'If you don't marry soon other girls will get all the men, you know.' She is coy about this.

A third says she and her husband would like me to meet their son, who has just bought a farm out Waingake way. They are sure he and I would make a good match.

Make a good match, my mind screams! Other girls will get all the men! Settle down with one of the locals! And men who professed love for me overseas write and also come and visit. What about it? Marriage? It would be easy to escape into an unreal world as S. did. And Min.

On a wet Anzac day I take my umbrella to the Cenotaph in a private sort of agony, and attend an RSA meeting at the drill hall afterwards, sitting in the front row. The secretary thanks me for coming and tells me my legs have been the only bright spot about the meeting. I smile as expected.

My parents know something is wrong, I am sure, know I am hiding something from them. Rightly or wrongly, I have no intention of telling them of the rape episode, or of Jock and Tone either.

As I sit on the verandah soaking up the sun and drinking yet another cup of tea a boy from the post office cycles through the gateway and up the long drive. Dropping his bicycle on the lawn by the steps, he smiles as he puts a hand into the brown leather bag hanging over his shoulder and passes me a handful of telegrams. My name has appeared in a list of 'Mentions in Despatches' awards.

Some telegrams are from New Zealand friends. Others come from my Clerical Division girls saying things like, 'Good show Dig' and 'Vivas from us all', and the stereotype message arrives from Mrs Jowett at Army Headquarters. There are telegrams, too, from men I met in Italy. My parents watch my reaction to these, but the messages are facetious or pedantic and convey nothing special.

Only one telegram my parents have not seen. The folded yellow form with its purple printing is hidden in a bedroom drawer. It reads: 'Congratulations Neve on a well deserved reward. Nothing changes. My love as always. Tone.'

It is hard to say how often I have read that telegram. Part of me wants to respond but I know I won't, because Tone and I made a pact that we will not write to each other. Acknowledging a decoration is special, and had he been listed in the newspaper I'd have telegraphed him as he has me, but I wouldn't have expected a reply any more than he will. We are both so loyal it is appalling.

Doing nothing as I wait for a reply from Wellington is trying, which my father senses as he and I admire the grapevine, counting the bunches hiding amongst the leaves.

'Are you all right, Nugget?' he asks suddenly, and I turn from the vine and cry against his shoulder, where I have wanted to be for a long time.

'All these kind people are driving me crazy, Dad. Tell me you understand there might be a reason I don't want to settle down and be married as everyone wants me to be. For God's sake tell me you understand.'

'Mum and I know something's wrong, Nugget, and it's hard to stand aside, but only you know how to deal with what that something is. We just want you to know we're here, as we were when Geoff was killed. We'll always be here for you.'

'I've banked on you, Dad. Over there. And now. I love you so much.' My father hands me his large white handkerchief and I blow my nose as I cry and cry.

In my bedroom I wonder how well I will cope with the type of tolerance I have never before needed, as I return to what I suppose is reality. I know I've had much that I've loved snatched from me, but I've also known more love than many others have, so perhaps things balance out somehow.

I look in the mirror and tell my reflection, 'In a mixed-up sort of way, you are a very rich young lady. Never forget that.'

Another day dawns and a telegram arrives with a date in it.

I run for my father who is outside pruning. 'This is what I've been waiting for. Look!'

My father reads the telegram. 'You're a bit of a dark horse. Let's tell Mum.'

We go inside and show the telegram to Mum, who is bent over her sewing machine making blue and white gingham curtains for the kitchen. She reads the message and raises her beautiful brown eyes. 'The Prime Minister's office!' she says.

She pushes back her chair, gives me a good hard look, then reaches for Dad's hand as she stands close to him, her height matching his. She says nothing.

What she has done is so ordinary, yet so unusual I am surprised. I have no idea what she is thinking, but it must be something special.

What my father does is not at all unexpected. He gives me what seems a very Irish wink, full of wickedness.

'I'll put the kettle on,' Mum says, smiling. 'We'll have a cup of tea.'

Now that, I think, is not at all surprising. How many cups of tea have I drunk since arriving home? Dozens? Hundreds?

'Lovely,' I say. And I think I mean it. Because this cup of tea is special. It isn't just any old cup of tea, is it? It's the first cup of tea in my new life, whatever that might be.